CAPITAL DILEMMA

CAPITAL DILEMMA

Germany's Search for a New Architecture of Democracy

Michael Z. Wise

Princeton Architectural Press, New York

Published by
Princeton Architectural Press
37 East 7th Street
New York, New York 10003
212.995.9620

For a free catalog of books, call 1.800.722.6657.
Visit our web site at www.papress.com.

Editing and design: Clare Jacobson
Index: Marty Jezer
Special thanks to: Eugenia Bell, Jane Garvie, Caroline
Green, Therese Kelly, Mark Lamster, Anne Nitschke,
and Sara E. Stemen of Princeton Architectural Press
—Kevin C. Lippert, publisher

Library of Congress Cataloging-in-Publication Data
Wise, Michael Z., 1957–
     Capital dilemma: Germany's search for a new
architecture of democracy / Michael Z. Wise.
          p.   cm.
     Includes bibliographical references and index.
     ISBN 1-56898-134-1
     1. Architecture and state—Germany—Berlin.
2. National socialism and architecture—Germany
—Berlin. 3. Architecture, Modern—20th century
—Germany—Berlin. 4. Berlin (Germany)—
Buildings, structures, etc. I. Title.
NA1085.W58 1998
725'.0943'15507444361—DC21   97-45030
                                        CIP

Endsheets
Front: Model of Albert Speer's proposed north-south
axis for Berlin (never realized), 1938, photo courtesy
Landesbildstelle Berlin.
Back: Federal Strip designed by Axel Schultes and
Charlotte Frank, the winning entry in postunification
Berlin's Spreebogen competition, photo courtesy Axel
Schultes Architekten.

CONTENTS

To my parents,
Bobbi and Zelig Wise

If anyone inquires about the higher authority that directs everything, it is never to be found in one spot. . . . We are afraid of a capital.

—Goethe, *Wilhelm Meisters Wanderjahre*

Like stories written in stone, capitals across the globe embody national identity and historical consciousness. Be it the Mall in Washington, D.C., the Kremlin in Moscow, or the Forbidden City in Beijing, capital city buildings and urban planning have the power to awe, to alienate, to inspire, and to intimidate. But possibly no nation is more attuned to the political manipulation of built imagery than Germany. The decision to move its government seat from Bonn to Berlin by the year 2000 has set off a remarkable debate about what kind of official architecture is appropriate for a country whose past has rendered patriotism suspect and whose expressions of national pride have, as a result, been consigned to the soccer field. The impassioned, often vituperative, discussion about the redesign of Berlin following the fall of communism offers a valuable lens through which to consider Germany's future direction and its relationship to the past.

Modern German cities, Adolf Hitler lamented in *Mein Kampf*, lack monumental architecture and potent symbols of nationhood. Hitler set out to remedy this by transforming Berlin into "Germania," a capital worthy of his Thousand Year Reich. Immediately after the 1940 conquest of Paris, he announced plans to rebuild Berlin in a "style commensurate with the grandeur of our victory."[1] His architect, Albert Speer, had already drawn up a vast north-south axis, a *via triumphalis* for the Führer of Europe and beyond. For one end of the never-realized scheme, a soaring domed hall was proposed. Its cavernous interior was so large—accommodating up to 180,000 people—that the architect anticipated the problem of clouds forming beneath the vaulted ceiling. Speer envisioned at the boulevard's other terminus a victory arch more than twice the size of the Arc de Triomphe.

Over half a century after Nazism's demise, democratic Germany fittingly selected Paris as the place to open a major exhibition about the latest architectural recreation of Berlin. The array of models and drawings projected how the metropolis would look at the dawn of the next millennium. This unusual public relations exercise conveyed not just images and information about the new buildings of the once-and-future capital, but an explicit diplomatic message as well. "The exhibition strives to make clear that German policy will not change as a result of the move from Bonn to Berlin," wrote Building Minister Klaus Töpfer in the brochure distributed to visitors.[2]

The attempt to reassure Germany's neighbors about the historic transfer highlights the significance Germans attach to the link between architecture and politics. Indeed, Germany has assigned architecture a pivotal role throughout its turbulent twentieth-century history. Prior to its successive rule by the century's warring ideologies, Nazism and communism, Germany gave birth to the Bauhaus movement, whose founders argued that their own revolutionary designs could shape human destiny. Other pioneering German architects, like Bruno Taut and Wassily Luckhardt, devised elaborate crystalline structures they regarded as moral beacons of a shining future. Convulsive events like the fall of the monarchy in 1918, Hitler's rise to power in 1933, and the defeat of his Third Reich in 1945 all have left their mark on German architecture and design. "Time and again it was to be made clear in stone that from now on everything was to be different," a postwar architect wrote of the repeated stylistic changes.[3]

How will the official architecture of unified Berlin, a democratic capital being built amid totalitarian remains, be different this time around? That question, and the various strategies the Germans have devised to address it, are the subject of this book. Several writers have examined the political underpinnings of earlier twentieth-century German state architecture. Many others have analyzed modern Germany in political or economic terms. But this book offers the first overview of the postwar and now postunification effort by the democratic German state to present itself in built form. The transfer of the Bundestag (the national legislature) and leading government bodies to Berlin poses an epic design challenge, a capital dilemma at the root of which lie the painful memories of past regimes. Berlin is haunted by its history as font of Prussian militarism, seat of a failed bid at democracy under the Weimar Republic, headquarters of genocidal Nazi rule, and the cold-war fault line between East and West. In its latest incarnation, Berlin will become the capital of the fifth German state in this century to be ruled from that city. The Federal Republic of Germany, a highly stable democracy in stark contrast to its predecessors, has been struggling with their burdensome architectural legacies. In the process, it has considered remedies as varied as outright destruction, refurbishment, and, in the case of the former Nazi central bank now being converted into the new Foreign Ministry, physical concealment.

The demolition plans stemmed partly from an aversion to occupying buildings created by dictatorial regimes. But West German officials moving to Berlin were also loath to accept any sacrifice in the quality of office space compared to that they occupied in Bonn. They doubted that the drab, aging governmental properties that came under the Federal Republic's control after the demise of East Germany would provide efficient and comfortable quarters. An initial inspection of the premises confirmed their suspicions. "I asked myself if it were thinkable that the ruling class of an industrial nation would use such toilets," senior Finance Ministry official Hans-Michael Meyer-Sebastian told me. "The conditions were dreadful."[4] The ministry eventually found it easy enough to upgrade the antiquated plumbing. Muting the militaristic tenor of its future home, Hermann Göring's former Luftwaffe Headquarters, has proven a more difficult challenge. Germany's desire to embody the image of a liberal democratic polity in Berlin's new buildings, like the offices for the federal president—the head of state—and the Chancellery, which houses working quarters for the government chief, posed a separate formidable task.

As illustrated by the state-sponsored Paris exhibition, today's Germany is at pains to assuage anyone casting a skeptical eye towards Berlin, soon to be capital of a country of 82 million people and Europe's undisputed powerhouse. Unification restored the population and territory governed from Berlin to roughly their size prior to World War II, turning the page on a national partition little regretted elsewhere on the continent. France regarded Germany's division as an important constraint on its power. The author François Mauriac memorably observed that he loved Germany so much he was glad there were two of them,[5] and since 1989 many Europeans have harbored fears about a German resurgence, nowadays focusing more on the economic than the military realm. Germans too have worried about a revival of their own nationalist demons. Chancellor Helmut Kohl proffered integration with the European Union as the best antidote, a way to subsume his countrymen in a larger entity and thereby save them from themselves. The success of the venture, he ominously warned, was a question of "war and peace in the twenty-first century."[6]

As they have negotiated tethering their fate to that of their fellow Europeans, German authorities have been grappling to find a design vocabulary that will turn its back on the monumentality typical of their history's most worrisome periods. At the same time, they desire structures deemed worthy of a cosmopolitan capital and conducive to the urban scale and traditions of Berlin. There have been other major national capital projects in this century—Brasilia, New Delhi, Ankara, and Canberra are some examples—but perhaps never before has an endeavor of this kind been carried out with such anxiety about architectural symbolism.

"Political places . . . are not randomly or casually brought into existence," political scientist Charles T. Goodsell writes in his study of political meaning in architecture. For these spaces are embedded with key clues about a nation's power structure and nonverbal commentary about its people and civilization.[7]

The new Berlin will be filled with spaces of this kind. Planning them, German officials have weighed many concerns—among them, budget constraints, environmental protection, historic preservation, efficiency, and comfort—all of which are intertwined with the issue of symbolism. The officials vowed early on in the planning process that there would be no revival of Speer's megalomaniacal schemes, of the grandiose air of old Prussian ministries, or of Wilhelmine pomposity. But vague yearnings also emerged for something more demonstrative than the post-war West German government seat. Bonn's image as a faint-hearted capital doubtless played a role in the subconscious of many representatives who voted in favor of moving back to Berlin, argued Bundestag member Peter Glotz. For capitals are not only workplaces but stages for the visualization of power. As such, Bonn was "too practical, too realistic, and too average to satisfy the resurgent longing for history, for pathos, and for dignity."[8]

In response to Speer's overblown neoclassicism for Nazi Berlin, the Federal Republic based in Bonn studiously downplayed architectural grandeur. Government ministries embarked upon a new era in the small town along the Rhine by operating from unassuming, makeshift quarters. German government chiefs from Ludwig Erhard to Kohl have occupied a squat, clean-lined official residence with the lowly label of "Kanzlerbungalow" (Chancellor's Bungalow). The modern Parliament Building was designed with similar restraint. A low-rise pavilion, it contains a circular plenary chamber devised to avoid any trace of hierarchy. The facade features much transparent glass to express openness and accessibility. Such symbolic use of clear glass flourished as the primary tenet in designing prestigious official West German structures.

A closer look at history and comparisons of state buildings under highly disparate political systems makes it difficult to sustain an automatic congruence between architectural form and ideological content. Keeping in mind the frequent use of glass as an emblem for democratic transparency in Bonn, consider the Italian avant-garde architecture built under Benito Mussolini's reign. Giuseppe Terragni sought to symbolize the Italian fascist movement in his 1932 design for the Casa del Fascio (House of Fascism) in Como. "Here is the Mussolinian concept that fascism is a glass house into which everyone can peer, giving rise to the architecture that is the complement of this idea: no encumbrance, no barrier, no obstacle between the political hierarchy and the people," Terragni said, injecting his own politics into form.[9]

Yet, despite the stylistic parallels in political systems of widely divergent ideologies, architecture can clearly express political meaning. Goodsell has noted for example that Hitler's Reich Chancellery office was more than a thousand square feet larger than the British House of Commons chamber. "The Reich Chancellery, with its incredible longitudinal dimensions and blatant symbolism, speaks volumes about the imperious nature of the Nazi state and the megalomania of its head. Just as articulately, the dimensions and the intimacy of the House of Commons say much about the British penchant for face-to-face political debate."[10]

What signals will be sent by the official architecture of the new Berlin? Even if the postwar city long remained but a shadow of its former self, Berlin's axial boulevards and surviving monumental buildings offer a far grander stage than Bonn upon which to raise the curtain for German history's next act. A leading architectural advisor to Chancellor Kohl, former Federal Building Board president Barbara Jakubeit, argued that the electorate was ready for an architectural setting quite different from Bonn. "The citizens want their government to be located in a fixed place, not hidden in sackcloth and ashes. They want to be proud," she said, before quickly catching herself. "Perhaps not proud. But they don't want the government to have to creep away into any old mouse hole."[11]

Jakubeit's apparent concern about being misunderstood, coupled with her desire for Germany to move on, arose time and again in the debate about state architecture and what it says about Germany's broader direction. Such a keen sensitivity to potential foreign criticism of design gestures as a bellwether of renascent nationalism became second nature in Bonn. When a 1970s landscaping plan for the Chancellery there involved placing a large globelike sculpture in the forecourt, then-Chancellor Helmut Schmidt vetoed the scheme for fear that the work might be misinterpreted as a sign of renewed German international aspirations. An anodyne bronze by Henry Moore was chosen instead, and the ill-conceived globe ended up in an out-of-the-way spot near the Rhine's edge, where it still sits, threatening no one.

After Germany was reunified, some grew impatient with this kind of ingrained hesitancy. "In the capital of the most economically powerful country in Europe we cannot act as if we were a small banana republic," said Bundestag Vice President Hans Klein, decrying the design philosophy behind the low-key Bonn Parliament Building as a "form of subservience" to the Allied powers who occupied the country in 1945.[12] Kohl's former Building Minister Oscar Schneider was another advocate of trading unobtrusive Bonn for a more expressive capital. "We Germans must finally take off this tattered Cinderella's dress and find our way back to a healthy self-confidence," he said.[13]

Michael Stürmer, a historian who served as an advisor to Kohl, called Bonn "the shamefaced capital of a shamefaced state" and bemoaned the unobtrusiveness of its architecture. "To some extent it was downright practical, particularly for motorists. But visitors from Rome, Washington, Paris, and Madrid had to be reminded from time to time that they were arriving at the center of a state and not on the grounds of an international insurance firm. . . . Now however the time has come, in matters of symbols, style, and architecture, to make up for what for forty years seemed superfluous because of the German past and the European future."[14]

Mathias Schreiber, the cultural editor of the weekly magazine *Der Spiegel*, also urged a bolder expression of Germany's power. "The unending Bonn inconspicuousness, timidity, and embarrassment, the tranquillity of the seemingly improvised, the box-like buildings strewn along the edges of the street—all of that is an inadequate representation, an unworthy form for a country that has regained its sovereignty. We should finally dare to be great again in our state architecture. The dream of representative buildings . . . is neither fascistic nor *Grossdeutsch*. It is as European as urban capitals like Vienna, Florence, Paris, London, Stockholm, and Berlin."[15]

For present-day Berlin to become a focal point for national sentiment like the capitals of other countries—normal and seemingly unburdened by history—was the goal of many conservative politicians and intellectuals. After unification they envisioned Germany entering a new stage in which it would attain a distanced relationship to its Nazi past. As the Third Reich receded from immediacy, they saw the subdued period of Bonn-based government being replaced by a more assertive, self-confident Berlin republic. Germany, according to this scenario, would more and more resemble other nations that were free to pursue their own interests. And in the years following unification, the country did begin slowly assuming international responsibilities commensurate with its political and economic weight. Foreign Minister Klaus Kinkel asked the United Nations to consider according Germany permanent membership in its Security Council. In 1996, the Bundestag voted by an overwhelming majority to send 2,000 soldiers to the Balkans as part of a UN peacekeeping force—the first time that German combat troops had been deployed abroad since World War II.

On the other side of the political spectrum, however, there was greater reluctance to take on these larger political responsibilities, and even less of a wish to project power through symbols like state architecture. Members of the German left preferred to see their country as a larger version of Switzerland or Austria. Pacifism and antinationalism, in their view, represented a proud postwar inheritance that could thwart a reprise of German hegemony. The opposition Social Democratic Party has generally resisted the deployment of German troops in the international arena. Some of its leading members worried that an abandonment of Bonn's subdued format carried future risks for themselves and their

European neighbors. "After 1945 we regained the friendship of other peoples, not with grandiosity, but with modesty," said a key player in Bonn's architectural development, the Social Democratic parliamentarian Peter Conradi. "No one ever feared Bonn. We don't want anyone to fear Berlin."[16]

Throughout the decades when Bonn served as provisional capital, planners searchingly asked whether there was an official architectural style best suited to open societies, and how building design in a democracy differed from that under totalitarianism. In Berlin, where dictatorial rule held sway for much of this century, these questions are being posed with a new urgency. At times, the answers have been superficial. Simplistic semiotic equations—like the notion that glass facades amount to political transparency—have been pursued with exaggerated rigor, and German politicians have often displayed a tendency to take the symbol for the reality itself.

Still, the Germans planning Berlin have found that the questions themselves will not go away, in part because of fear of what others might think about their responses, and in part out of their own confusion over who they have become in the aftermath of unification. To understand the official architecture of unified Berlin and the issues it raises, I interviewed many of the leading architects, politicians, and planners involved in creating the new capital. These interviews, along with historical research and contemporary accounts in the German press and in architectural journals, formed the basis of this book.

I begin with an examination of the unusual official architectural path followed by West Germany in Bonn, and of the very different course taken by the Communist government in East Berlin. After both of these capitals became outmoded as a result of unification, architects and planners rushed back to their drawing boards. The subsequent chapters examine the design of the new Chancellery and of new offices for the federal presidency; the awkward process of siting today's government ministries and other entities in the architectural remains of now extinct regimes; the restoration of the former imperial parliament, the Reichstag, as home to the federal legislature; and the creation of a memorial to commemorate past horrors and iniquities perpetrated from Berlin—each of them key components in Germany's effort to resolve its capital dilemma.

HEADQUARTERS FOR A DIVIDED NATION

Aside from the birth of Ludwig van Beethoven, who moved away as soon as he was old enough to do so, little of historical significance occurred in Bonn before May 10, 1949. Then, shortly before midnight, West German politicians proclaimed the tranquil Rhineland town to be their provisional capital. It was precisely this lack of history that made it so appealing. "Bonn was a beginning, a city without a past," recalled West Germany's founding Chancellor Konrad Adenauer.[17]

Governing from the historic capital of Berlin was out of the question for the time being since it was occupied by the World War II victors and encircled by a communist stronghold under Soviet control. The decision for Bonn came in a narrow vote of thirty-three to twenty-nine, taken by the West German Parliamentary Council, forerunner to the government of the Federal Republic of Germany. Compared to the alternative choice, the commercial and banking center of Frankfurt, sleepy Bonn was considered less likely to pose any claim to being more than a way station. This added to its allure in the eyes of those bent on reunifying the country and moving the government back to Berlin as soon as possible. A more prosaic factor also played a decisive role in Bonn's selection—Adenauer had a comfortable country house in a nearby village.

Bonn was an odd and implausible capital city, given the degree of power that came to be concentrated there. It did have a mid-sized university, but, unlike London or Paris, it boasted no major museum or cultural institution. Although its population swelled to 300,000 due to the influx of politicians, bureaucrats, lobbyists, journalists, and diplomats from around the globe, it never acquired cosmopolitan flair or urbanity during its nearly half a century as government seat. Some of these new residents found Bonn refreshingly quaint; many deemed it an excruciatingly dull backwater. The high-ranking visitors who came calling, a lengthy roster including u.s. presidents, European premiers, the queen of England, and the emperors of Iran, Ethiopia, and Japan, were accustomed to being received in far grander premises. "One of the strangest capitals of the twentieth century," commented the *New York Herald Tribune* when President Dwight D. Eisenhower paid a state visit in 1959.[18] During the 1960s, English envoys referred to the British Embassy in Bonn as "Her Majesty's only mission in a cornfield."[19] A *Newsweek* correspondent marveled how the magazine's news bureau, a block away from the federal Parliament, "faced a meadow on which a shepherd grazed his flock every Friday afternoon."[20]

Most Germans were initially quite satisfied to have such a low-key capital. Free of Berlin's architectural bombast, Bonn represented a reassuring sign of discontinuity in their troubled history. The symbolic image of the Federal Republic born out of the rubble of fascism was deliberately self-effacing—a renunciation of pretense that amounted to an architectural declaration of "never again." This design approach coincided with a concerted political drive to show that in its democratic reincarnation the fledgling West German state had forsworn all territorial ambitions and merited a return to the ranks of respectable nations. Towards this end, the Bonn government paid billions of dollars in reparations to Holocaust survivors and, under the tutelage of the Allied World War ii victors, adopted a severely limited, nonnuclear defense strategy. With astonishing rapidity, the vanquished country diligently rebuilt its infrastructure, developing into an economic giant but a political pygmy. West German politicians, chastened by the calamity of the Third Reich, invoked that self-description with contentment, not regret.

As in every aspect of postwar life, the new West German direction in public architecture followed the dramatic pendulum swing by which many believed—somewhat naively—that Nazism could be overcome by pursuing the opposite of what had until just recently prevailed. Politicians thus located the new national legislature, the Bundestag, inside a prime example of the Bauhaus architecture reviled by the Nazis. The Pädagogische Akademie, a former teachers' college, was a building of pure white planes set along the Rhine River south of the town center *(see figure 2)*. Designed by Martin Witte in 1930, its dedication in October 1933 came just months after Hitler took power and created the cultural climate in which a flat-roofed modernist structure like the Akademie could be called by Nazi propagandists "a child of other skies and other blood."[21] Bonn's Nazi mayor derided its architecture for contravening the "German character."[22] But in the dawning days of the Federal Republic, turning this building into a parliament was a signal of contrition and, like the choice of Bonn itself, a demonstrated desire for a new start.

West German leaders met temporarily in the academy's main assembly hall until architect Hans Schwippert, a colleague of Erich Mendelsohn and Mies van der Rohe prior to their flight into exile from the Nazis, added on a larger legislative chamber. The addition featured floor-to-ceiling transparent glass windows running sixty feet along two of its sides and was considered an apt metaphor for the political openness of the new democracy. Schwippert did not invent the link between architectural transparency and an accessible government. The idea dated from the early days of the Modern Movement. As the Bauhaus pioneer Hannes Meyer wrote of his design for the 1927 League of Nations Headquarters competition, "No back corridors for backstairs diplomacy but open glazed rooms for public negotiation of honest men."[23]

The Bonn legislative chamber contained seats for journalists, but it was not big enough to accommodate a public gallery, so temporary bleachers were erected outside. Seated there, spectators strained to follow the proceedings through the windows. Photographs taken at the Bundestag's inaugural session show crowds peering into Schwippert's building as if into an aquarium *(see figure 3)*. Some of the glass panels were left open to enable citizens to hear the debate going on inside. Light streamed through the clear panes, illuminating representatives of a citizenry who just a few years earlier had emerged from gloomy wartime bunkers.

"Politics is a dark affair. Let's see to it that we shed some light upon it," observed Schwippert. After twelve years of shadowy dictatorship, the cultivation of an enlightened participatory democracy was the order of the day, and Schwippert saw architecture as a means to achieve this goal. "I wanted the German public to observe parliamentary work," he said a few years after his design was finished. "I wanted a building of openness, an architecture of meeting and discussion."[24]

Comparing the austere Bonn building to the hulking Reichstag in Berlin, to which Germany's parliament will return in 1999, is like weighing a penitent's pup tent against a potentate's palace. Simplicity reigned throughout the Bundestag structure, including in the furnishings that Schwippert designed himself, in keeping with Witte's unadorned academy. Political intent could be read into these furnishings as well. All members of the parliament—from the Bundestag president and government ministers down to the rank-and-file deputies and their secretarial support staff—were provided with the same desk, chairs, and bureau. "Here again there is no borrowing from the past for the sake of prestige; instead there are lightweight devices that are functional and do not conceal," Schwippert said. In a period of postwar shortages and poverty, he steadfastly refused to provide public servants of the humbled nation with grandeur or glamour at the workplace. That, he insisted, could come only "when politics again attains exalted levels. In the meantime, my sense is that this should be a temporary building for a new beginning of political life in Germany."[25]

But the prevailing postwar antipathy to anything vaguely resembling Nazi-era design did not mean that all politicians were sympathetic to Schwippert's inventive solutions. The architect's ideas did not mesh perfectly with his clients' less clearly defined visions. For example, he proposed a circular seating arrangement in the plenary chamber with no speaker's podium; hierarchy would be eliminated by having all representatives speak from their own seats. Adenauer rejected this, preferring a more traditional legislature arranged along the lines of a lecture hall. A chancellor who would eventually campaign for office under the slogan "No experiments!" was naturally disinclined to test drive a circular parliament. "Dr. Adenauer . . . thinks that one should not resort to such radical innovations right at the inception of parliamentary work," a Chancellery aide wrote to Schwippert.[26] Though Schwippert's circular plan was defeated, his building was nonetheless highly unconventional for its day, and Bundestag members boasted that it was the world's first "modern" parliament. With time, the circular seating arrangement gained an unusual degree of acceptance in Germany. The Bundestag adopted it some four decades later when it moved into larger quarters in Bonn; four of Germany's provincial legislatures built after 1987 also employed the circular pattern in their own plenary chambers.

The West German government reaffirmed the symbolic return to Bauhaus tradition when it deployed a no-frills modern architecture as an instrument of political statecraft abroad as well as at home. In 1954, the Federal Republic was invited to participate in the 1958 Brussels World Exposition. "After the terrible occurrences, it was very difficult for Germany . . . to appear again within the framework of such an international event," said architect Egon Eiermann, who with his colleague Sep Ruf designed the West German Pavilion. "This country had burdened itself with so much guilt that it was very difficult to find the correct tone," Eiermann commented.[27] But he and Ruf hit the right note with a pavilion of eight interlocking cubes, simply framed in glass and steel. The previous time Germany took part in a world exhibition was the 1937 Paris show. There Albert Speer's aggressive pavilion consisted of a towering mass of fluted limestone crowned by a ferocious eagle. Hailing the vivid contrast at Brussels two decades later, the Paris newspaper *Le Figaro* called Eiermann and Ruf's design a sign that the Germans "have retreated from the colossal and returned to the quiet fold of good European children."[28] Eiermann repeated this success in another sensitive foreign commission, the new West German embassy in Washington, D.C. *(see figure 4)*. Completed in 1964, the mission resembled a stately ocean liner nestled against sloping terrain. Its glass facade was covered in an outer skin of delicate steel railings and wooden sun screens. The humanely proportioned diplomatic outpost projected a welcome spirit of modesty and unassuming elegance, a billboard image for a German state set on changing its ways.

Similar characteristics were in evidence at the official Chancellery residence in Bonn designed by Ruf and dedicated in 1964 *(see figure 5)*. Low-slung and glass-walled, the humbly dubbed Kanzlerbungalow (Chancellor's Bungalow) took Mies van der Rohe's German Pavilion at the 1929 World Exhibition in Barcelona as its inspiration. By reaching back to the Mies design, Ruf sought to give testimony to the Federal Republic's rededication to the democratic ideals of the Weimar Republic. He achieved a building of quiet distinction and style. The open plan and few visible supporting elements gave it a sense of weightlessness. Former Bauhaus director Walter Gropius called the residence a "first-class specimen of German architecture which is highly able to represent to the world the progressive spirit of the German people and their cultural efforts in this day and age."[29] The first chancellor to live there, Ludwig Erhard, delighted in its design and set great stock in its power to broadcast a message. "You will get to know me better by looking around this house, than you possibly will from listening to me give a political speech," he said.[30] But most other chancellors intensely disliked the travertine-floored abode. Adenauer quipped that the building "wouldn't even burn," a feat of which the Reichstag in Berlin had proven eminently capable.[31] Three years after its completion, Chancellor Kurt-Georg Kiesinger ordered the residence's sleek interior appointments replaced with cozier antiques, despite protests by Gropius and other leading architects that the alterations marred the unity of Ruf's design. Willy Brandt refused to move in at all during his term as government chief. His successor Helmut Schmidt restored the classic modern furnishings.[32]

Other branches of the West German government set up quarters in quaint old villas that dotted the Bonn countryside. The presidency was housed in the Villa Hammerschmidt, built by a German industrialist in

1863 on a site just up the river from where the Bundestag held its sessions. Adenauer adapted another former private residence, the Palais Schaumburg, as his Chancellery; he borrowed furniture and paintings from the nearby city of Cologne to decorate its executive offices. Using existing properties and, for a time, even stopgap accommodations like rustic barracks left over from the war was thought to be the most fitting setup for a provisional capital, betokening the official determination to return to Berlin.

West Germany's rehabilitation of Bauhaus design helped create a palatable new national cultural identity since so many other areas of the German artistic legacy were tainted by association with Nazism. The official canonization of what had become a transatlantic architectural idiom also gave expression to the cold-war partnership between the Federal Republic and the United States, where Gropius, Mies, Marcel Breuer, and other Bauhaus veterans had found a haven from fascism.[33] Their success in reestablishing themselves there was so great that Bauhaus–inspired modernism became the house style for corporate America in the late 1950s and 1960s, a period when Washington itself turned to the avatars of the International Style to design a series of new u.s. embassies abroad.

Before the war, Berlin had been not only the governmental capital but also the economic, industrial, and military center of Germany. In response to this, West Germans preferred locating some official entities outside the new government seat as part of a consciously decentralized federated structure. The Bundesbank, the central bank, was established not in Bonn but in Frankfurt. The Federal Constitutional Court, the supreme judicial arbiter, deliberated in Karlsruhe in another modern glass–walled structure. The Federal Crime Agency, the German equivalent of the fbi, sat in Wiesbaden. Whereas Berlin had dominated many aspects of German life, such as the media and the arts, these too became dispersed in the Federal Republic. Hamburg developed as the editorial headquarters for many national news publications, while cultural institutions of national importance arose in cities like Munich and Düsseldorf.

This decentralized format was echoed in the shaping of the capital itself. An aversion to large-scale planning schemes following the Nazi debacle led to a haphazard placement of government entities according to what, owing to Bonn's pastoral calm, was described as a "cows in the pasture" school of urban layout. The government district arose helter-skelter in the vast open fields and sparsely populated residential areas south of the compact, tidy town center around the old university. This district was nicknamed "Spaceship Bonn," for it seemed to have arrived suddenly from a distant planet onto the Rhineland's *tabula rasa*, liberated from any contextual constraints or historical precedent. Politicians and bureaucrats tended to leave the area deserted on weekends and other periods outside of parliamentary sessions.

In the 1950s, when Germany began to recover from the war and its "economic miracle" was under way, it was becoming clear that Bonn's status as capital was not so temporary after all. West German politicians' pretense of sitting on packed suitcases ready to abandon Bonn at a moment's notice was belied by a building boom that responded to the basic day-to-day needs of a modern government bureaucracy. Other than using a second-rate variant of the modern idiom, little thought was paid to the actual appearance of many ministries. The volume of new construction was inconsistent with Bonn's ethos of design restraint. As West Germany became an increasingly important player in the North Atlantic Treaty Organization during the cold war, "provisional" could hardly describe the sprawling complexes built to house key government agencies. A boxy new Foreign Ministry Building loomed over the Rhine; locals dubbed the expansive Defense Ministry Headquarters the "Pentabonn." Parts of the capital seemed to reflect democracy with a barely human face. Anxious to avoid an unwelcome revival of monumentality, an evasively bland functionality held sway, as if by default.

The erection of the Berlin Wall in 1961 put an end to any illusions that unification was on the horizon, and so had an impact on Bonn's development. The modest scale used in prestige projects like the

Bundestag and the Kanzlerbungalow was most conspicuously flouted in 1966 when parliamentary deputies, weary of the lack of permanent office space in Bonn, constructed a twenty-nine-story office building for themselves and their committees *(see figure 6)*. The tower constituted the first major vertical landmark on the Bonn skyline. Drawn up by Egon Eiermann, its bulk was overlaid in a simple filigree of steel and wood sun shades like that used in his Washington Embassy. But this design was vastly overscaled for its environs, and the lightweight outer skin failed to mask the building's excessive volume. The building became known as "Langer Eugen" (Tall Eugen)—a Germanic counterpart to London's Big Ben—after Bundestag President Eugen Gerstenmaier, during whose tenure it was constructed. The evolving architecture seemed to contradict the vow to return to Berlin. John le Carré noted the jumble in his 1968 thriller *A Small Town in Germany*, set partly in Bonn, the anomalous capital whose buildings he described as "discreetly temporary in deference to the dream, discreetly permanent in deference to the reality."[34]

Even more fundamental change came in 1969, when the newly elected Chancellor Willy Brandt began pursuing *Ostpolitik*, détente with Eastern Europe, including East Germany. Brandt argued that while there was one German "nation," this did not preclude the existence of two German states that might at some future date unify peacefully. The earlier rhetoric about a return to Berlin was decidedly toned down. With Brandt's government seeking to coexist with the Communists and reduce tensions between the two Germanys, the chancellor opted for a pragmatic resolution of his own shortage of office space and undertook construction of Bonn's first purpose-built Chancellery Headquarters *(see figure 7)*. It was willfully nondescript. When a design by the Planungsgruppe Stieldorf was chosen out of forty-six proposals, *Der Spiegel* commented that it was "the plainest of them all."[35]

Many critics thought the bland sobriety of the new Chancellery, completed in 1976, took understatement too far. Sheathed in clear glass and dark bronze-colored aluminum panels, its facade looked little different from any corporate office for BMW or Siemens. Its first occupant, Helmut Schmidt, found that the dull three-story structure had all the charm of a savings bank. It acquired neither an iconic presence in the media nor came to be synonymous with the government chief's position in the manner of the White House or 10 Downing Street. "I certainly did not expect when I first saw it that this was the place where the most powerful country in Europe has its headquarters," the American architect I. M. Pei said after a visit.[36] Far more prominent on the Bonn skyline was the rotating Daimler-Benz emblem atop a new commercial office building across the road from the Chancellery. In the minds of many Germans, this was a more fitting symbol of the Federal Republic's true self-image based on financial stability and material comfort.

But as West Germany grew in economic stature in the 1970s, disappointment arose over the numbing mediocrity of most official architecture in Bonn. Increasingly, there were calls to give the capital a more dignified public facade. Bonn's baroque Town Hall was the most architecturally significant building around, lamented President Walter Scheel at a dinner for the cabinet in 1977. Tourists looked in vain for signs that the slow-paced municipality was the government seat of a leading nation, he said, finding nothing but an array of everyday office buildings that, when examined at closer range, were adorned at their entryways with the federal eagle and a plaque indicating that such and such a ministry was housed there. Imploring government ministers to give the town a more coherent official visage, the president said, "There is a definite connection between Bonn's expansion and the credibility of our democracy; a credibility upon which ultimately our collective freedom depends. Architecture is also a language and I believe that we politicians must ensure that this language, like the language of politics in general, does not become empty jargon that no one wants to see or hear."[37]

As the Communist government in East Berlin and its Wall did not appear ready to vanish, politicians of the economically resurgent Federal Republic seemed intent on taking a new design tack in Bonn. In 1979,

Bundestag President Richard Stücklen called for the construction of a new Parliament to replace Schwippert's increasingly cramped refurbished teachers' college. "A democratic state also needs a certain splendor to be attractive," he said. "Only a state with a dignified and confident self-image can enjoy the respect and affection of its citizens."[38] His request signaled a recognition by some politicians that the restrained architecture of Bonn's early years was insufficient to promote a much-needed sense of civic belonging and a healthy form of national identity.

Moves in this direction were made by building major cultural institutions to line the Adenauerallee/Friedrich-Ebert-Allee, the main thoroughfare of Bonn's governmental district. In order to elevate the cultural life of the hum-drum town and display postwar Germany's artistic prowess, the government added the vast Bonn City Art Museum, designed by Axel Schultes, and the Art and Exhibition Hall of the Federal Republic of Germany, designed by Gustav Peichl, an Austrian architect close to Chancellor Helmut Kohl. The German Museum of Contemporary History, the work of Ingeborg and Hartmut Rüdiger, was also built along the same thoroughfare, adding a blatant air of previously abjured permanence with its beige granite walls and vaulted roof of steel and glass. Had anyone foreseen East Germany's demise, these large-scale, multimillion dollar projects never would have been put on the drawing board. They were completed after the collapse of the Wall and opened amid concern that they were rapidly destined to become expensive white elephants when the government transferred its operations to Berlin.

The costly new Bundestag plenary chamber that replaced Schwippert's legislative hall was the victim of even worse timing. After much hesitation, politicians agreed in the late 1980s to tear down the 1949 chamber to make way for a more commodious structure by the Stuttgart-based architect Günter Behnisch, who sees himself as heir to the design legacy of Schwippert, Eiermann, and Ruf (*see figure 8*). Like them, Behnisch has pronounced ideas about what architecture can achieve and the way a democracy should embody itself in its official structures. His architectural outlook stems from his personal history. Born in 1922, he joined the Hitler Youth as an adolescent and later became a U-boat commander before ending up as a prisoner of war in Great Britain. In the wake of Nazism's defeat, he dedicated himself to designing its antithesis. For him, monumental facades, stony symmetry, and long axes evoke jack-booted soldiers; and behind rows of columns lurk blood-spattered tyrants.

His practice, known as Behnisch & Partners, acquired international prominence for its contribution to the 1972 Olympic Games stadia in Munich. Although that athletic event was overshadowed by the Palestinian terrorist slaying of Israeli sportsmen, organizers had hoped it would be remembered for Behnisch's festive and playful tent-roof constructions, designed with the architect Frei Otto by stretching transparent textiles over a cable-net frame. The gossamer lightness of these constructions presented a demonstrative counterpoint to the previous Olympic Games held on German soil, the 1936 Berlin event presided over by Hitler at a classically inspired stadium of heavy stone. The totalitarian nation that put itself on view at the Berlin games was supplanted in Munich by a far more relaxed and neighborly Germany.

Behnisch believes that architecture sends distinct signals about the nature of the society in which it is designed. "When democratic conditions prevail at the time architecture comes into being, democratic architecture must arise," he said. And he, much like Schwippert, is unwilling to glorify politicians with state architecture, insisting on using it instead to help nurture the democratic process itself and combat forces he sees as threatening]it—excessive wealth, political party control, and personal ambition. "We must regulate the powers that push their way into architecture. Inappropriate ambitions must be nipped in the bud, thwarted, and reduced. And the weak, who are perhaps more worthy, should be strengthened," he said.[39]

In this respect, Behnisch tells a story about Frederick the Great. Annoyed at the grating rattle of a windmill sited near his palace of Sans Souci, the Prussian king commanded that the mill be torn down. Its owner took the matter to a court, which ruled that the clattering machinery could remain in operation despite royal displeasure. "We are like the windmiller," Behnisch proclaimed, clearly proud of the reaction his buildings provoke among leaders of democratic Germany.[40] His low-rise modernist Parliament for Bonn constantly reminds politicians who work in it that not they, but the voters, are sovereign. Staircases are set off-angle to mute their grandeur and, lest politicians be tempted to undemocratic heights, the steps lead down rather than up to the modestly appointed chamber. Instead of high-minded lapidary inscriptions, playful poetry has been painted on the clear glass walls. Only the red, black, and gold national flag flying outside, alongside the banner of the European Union, and the door handles, imprinted with the image of the federal eagle, signal that this is an official building.

Like the old teachers' college—preserved as home to the smaller upper house of parliament known as the Bundesrat—Behnisch's new architecture for the Bundestag poses a stark contrast to the bullying overblown classicism deployed by Speer for the Third Reich. Instead of marble or granite, Behnisch installed raw concrete floors at the entry. Where the concrete floors are covered, there are natural sisal runners rather than plush red carpets. The unassuming effect confused some visitors who in 1990s Germany expected something more august. "Many of our guests say, 'Oh, it's not finished yet.'" said Gabrielle Gödeken, a tour guide at the Parliament, several months after the building's dedication.

The concrete floors are not the only jarring feature in some visitors' eyes. There are no soaring pillars to recall Speer, but instead the flat roof sits upon steel gray I-beams. The array of metal and glass prompted some to liken the entrance of the building to an airport departure hall or a train station. "What was intended as criticism is praise," said Peter Conradi, a parliamentarian who was a key supporter of Behnisch's design. "The building opens itself up to visitors, to school groups. The Parliament Building does not intimidate, rather it invites curiosity. The people are welcome in the house of their representatives."[41] The industrial elements of the building were similarly lauded by Bundestag President Rita Süssmuth for reinforcing the German parliament's image as a "laboratory of democracy."[42]

The metaphor of expansive glass walls for democratic transparency was repeated here, though the panels were bullet-proofed for security. A large spectator gallery and press tribune inside the plenary chamber eliminates the need for bleachers like those erected outside Schwippert's building. Of course, the reality is such that many of the Bundestag's key political decisions are made not in the clear-paneled chamber but in back-room negotiations and closed committee meetings. The glass walls do ensure the legislators dramatic views out to the Rhine, in effect giving the modern parliament a natural backdrop celebrated in ancient Teutonic lore, the poetry of Heinrich Heine, and the operas of Richard Wagner.

But the light-filled chamber hardly has the pathos traditionally beloved of German culture. It communicates an open and friendly character. There is a Japanese lightness to the place; a Behnisch-designed annex housing the offices of the Bundestag president and vice presidents contains sliding translucent shoji screens instead of curtains to grant some privacy in the riverbank offices. The legislature's circular seating arrangement, which Adenauer thwarted in Schwippert's design, is intended to signal the cooperative will within a democracy *(see figure 9)*. Its form embodies, in Behnisch's view, an antiauthoritarian forum devoid of hierarchical arrangements in which all parliamentarians are seated at the same level. Here no one can deliver a dressing-down from on high.

The chamber's focal point is a massive aluminum eagle affixed to the wall behind the Bundestag president's seat. Selected after considerable Bundestag debate, this eagle looks less vigorous than that used on the emblems of the German federal army or presidency. The Bundestag bird tends toward the plump side and seems more like an imposing but amiable chicken than the aggressive high-flier of Germany's past. "Eagle-Lite" was how some parliamentarians referred to it when reviewing the ornithological alternatives.

Behnisch avoided strong colors and rich materials in favor of light blues and beige. Pale woods like maple, pine, ash, and oak were used for the balustrades, some flooring areas, and wall panels. The gradations in the shade of blue fabric covering the legislators' seats, Behnisch stated, aim to illustrate the array of opinions within a democracy. His fear of uniformity is also evident in the furnishings of lounge areas, which include a selection of armchairs and couches designed by celebrated modernists like Mies van der Rohe, Alvar Aalto, Eero Saarinen, Marcel Breuer, and Le Corbusier. The sheer diversity gives parts of the Bundestag the feeling of a well-stocked department store showroom.

Among the artworks in the building, there is not a figurative piece to be found, for fear of evoking the specter of heroic images favored by the Nazis. Foreign artists, including the American painter Sam Francis and sculptor Mark di Suvero, outnumber the Germans whose works are on view. Nicola de Maria's wildly colorful murals cover the walls and ceilings of the representatives' restaurant and bar. The art selection, like the restrained aura of the building in general, can be seen as a visible transmutation of the nationalist declaration "Deutschland, Deutschland über Alles!" into "Germany, Germany—among other things," a preferred alternative put forth by the leftist poet and essayist Hans Magnus Enzensberger.[43]

In the visitors' area on a lower level of the building, a series of panels elucidate some of the thinking behind the Bundestag architecture and the forces that shaped Bonn as a capital. The permanent exhibition seeks to prompt visitors to ponder Behnisch's symbol-packed legislature. It also provides comparative illustrations of other structures like the Palace of the Republic in Berlin, built to house Communist East Germany's rubber-stamp parliament, and fascist-era buildings like the House of German Art by Paul Ludwig Troost in Munich and the tribune designed by Speer for Nazi Party rallies in Nuremberg. "Columns do not stand for dictatorship, nor glass for democracy," the inscription on one panel reads. "Architecture in a democracy need not be faceless. Architecture in a democracy should be diverse, not pompous; self-confident, not bombastic; modest but not cheap. . . . To build in a democracy means to build for and with the citizens, not against them."

The statements have a dogmatic ring. That it was deemed necessary to explicitly articulate them inside a structure intended as their apotheosis indicates that Bonn's symbolic architecture is perhaps not as self-evident as Schwippert, Behnisch, and their kind might have hoped. All the same, many German politicians cling to these democratic symbols as if to articles of faith. Though not always consistently implemented in Bonn, they formed its unwritten architectural credo. The move back to Berlin put the credo to the test.

State architecture took an entirely different course in East Berlin, capital of the German Democratic Republic. Although they might have been expected to share Bonn's postwar antipathy to architectural grandeur, the East German Communists followed Moscow's lead in adopting a monumentalism intended to glorify their efforts to forge a new society.

A year after East Germany's founding in 1949, Walter Ulbricht, the leader of the Communist Party (formally known as the Socialist Unity Party of Germany), appealed for the creation of "monumental buildings to express the power and strength of Germany's great future." But he made clear that style, rather than scale alone, was a key criterion. "We do not want to see any more American boxes or buildings in Hitlerian barracks style in Berlin."[44] In language surprisingly similar to that invoked by the Nazis just a few years earlier, the Communists called for an architecture "comprehensible to the German *Volk* and corresponding to its national character."[45]

By stressing its devotion to Germany's classical tradition, the Communist regime presented itself as the authentic guardian of the national heritage in contrast to the "cultural barbarism" and "cosmopolitanism" pursued by the capitalist world. The charged vocabulary—"cosmopolitanism" was both Stalin's *bête noire* and a familiar Nazi term for "Jewish"—was invoked at a time when Moscow aspired to make Berlin the capital not just of the German Democratic Republic but of Germany as a whole, reunited in accordance with Soviet principles. In the process architecture became a tool of class warfare that would distinguish communist society and set its citizens apart from Western influences. In its premiere issue, *Deutsche Architektur*, the journal of the new East German Architectural Academy, painted a stark contrast with West Germany, where it said "buildings are being erected in an unpatriotic mode of formalism; a brutal, mendacious 'global style' of American coinage. . . . The deep differences in architectural development correspond to fundamental differences between the progressive policy of the German Democratic Republic and the reactionary policy in the Western part of our land."[46] The Communist condemnation of the Bauhaus style favored by the United States and the Federal Republic conveniently ignored its German origins. "The newly built, so-called Federal Building in Bonn is as lacking in Germanness as the policies of Adenauer," the official journal wrote of the Schwippert-Witte Parliament.[47]

While the West Germans governed from a Bauhaus box on Bonn's leafy riverbank, the East German government laid claim to the historic power center of both Prussia and the 1871-1918 German Empire. It did so since this part of Berlin fell within the Soviet zone of occupation. The area comprised the city's grandest pre-Nazi buildings, including the former Hohenzollern Royal Palace, the Berlin Cathedral, the university, and the art museums—all in various states of bomb-inflicted disrepair after the war.

A mammoth new Soviet Embassy arose in the midst of the wreckage, heralding the course that East German architecture was to follow in the early years of the self-styled "first workers' and peasants' state on German soil." The embassy was set along Berlin's main boulevard, Unter den Linden, taking up the same property used as Russia's diplomatic outpost since early nineteenth-century tsarist rule and spilling onto an adjacent plot previously occupied by a hotel. Construction got underway in 1949, using a historicist design that was the work of a Soviet team headed by Anatoli Stryschevski. The building's size and magnificence reflected the watershed finality of Stalin's victory over Hitler. It had fluted pillars, a rusticated stone base, carved balustrades, and other neoclassical decorations that brought to mind Moscow's lavish subway stations and wedding-cake-like administrative towers. A large marble bust of Lenin was erected in the embassy forecourt.

After this embassy was completed, the East Germans readily took their design cues from Moscow. In 1950, the East Berlin Communists sent a delegation of architects and construction functionaries to the Soviet Union. The delegation, led by Building Minister Lothar Bolz, toured Leningrad, Kiev, and Stalingrad and observed the annual May Day celebration on Moscow's Red Square. What they saw and heard from their Soviet comrades during a visit of over four weeks formed the basis of a document known as the "Sixteen Principles of Urban Planning," which the East German government adopted as a blueprint for future design. The principles were a rejoinder to the modernist planning techniques then in vogue in the West. They stressed that the socialist urban streetscape was not merely the province of vehicular traffic but a place of celebration and a means of elevating mass consciousness. The heart of the city was to be the political center, a place where monumental buildings would predominate and where the significance of the masses could be underscored through demonstrations, parades, and popular festivals. "In its structure and architectural form," the document proclaimed, "the city is the expression of political life and the national consciousness of the people."[48]

The East Germans put the new architectural directives into practice for the first time when they built the Stalinallee, a broad tree-lined boulevard of palatial apartment houses, constructed in part out of the wartime rubble (see figure 10). Modernism was resoundingly rejected in favor of a Socialist Realist style with a local flavor. Designs from great German architects of the eighteenth and nineteenth centuries, like Georg Wenzelaus von Knobelsdorff and Karl Friedrich Schinkel, were reclaimed for the proletariat. Window formats along the Stalinallee were based on Schinkel's Feilner Haus, a grand private residence destroyed by Allied bombing. Columns were derived from the Grosse Neugierde, a circular pavilion also designed by Schinkel at Schloss Glienicke near Potsdam. The facades were partially clad in stone and decorated with cream-colored Meissen ceramic tiles. In the new era, the Communists argued, architecture that was previously the preserve of the aristocracy and the bourgeoisie would henceforth be accorded the working class. "The time is gone forever when a privileged few lived in palaces, while shoe-box-like structures of spittle and ash were deemed good enough for the workers," declared an East Berlin magazine.[49]

At first, some East German architects were disinclined to design in the historicist mode. Hermann Henselmann, who before the war had favored a Corbusier-inspired modernism, tried to continue in that vein, but he soon found his work denounced as "formalist" and himself personally condemned for failing "to respond to the working-class sensibility."[50] But Henselmann quickly learned the ropes and delivered designs more pleasing to the regime. These included his Frankfurter Tor, a pair of twin towers forming a gateway along the Stalinallee (see figure 11), which drew on a trusted German historical precedent, Carl von Gontard's eighteenth-century towers flanking Schinkel's theater on a favored Berlin square, the Gendarmenmarkt. Shortly before his death in 1995 at age ninety, Henselmann conceded that the grandiose designs of the Stalinallee, renamed Karl-Marx-Allee after the denunciation of Stalin's personality cult, had brought "us in close proximity to Nazi architecture."[51]

Intent on resolving the acute postwar housing shortage in ruined Berlin, the East German government gave priority to the creation of new dwellings rather than to new official administrative buildings. Party and state functionaries, for the time being at least, made do with existing structures as their work quarters. The party-controlled media put its spotlight on the construction of new housing, giving prominent coverage to the Stalinallee. Agitprop events celebrated the project. Films, posters, poems, songs, and parades hailed the rebuilding of a new, transformed Berlin.

The communist leaders aspired to eventually build their own totems of power to replace vestiges of previous political systems. They also needed a vast expanse for the periodic mass rallies that were an integral part of communist state ritual as recently witnessed by the party's architectural delegation in Moscow. The Lustgarten, the public garden adjacent to the palace that Hitler had had paved over as a parade ground, was insufficient for these ceremonial affairs. To provide more room, the war-damaged Hohenzollern Royal Palace would have to cede its place. "The center of our capital, the Lustgarten and the site of the palace ruins, must become a great demonstration ground where the will of our people to fight and reconstruct can find expression," Ulbricht told a Communist Party Congress.[52]

In September 1950, less than four months after the delegation's return from the Soviet capital, demolition of the palace began despite vehement protests by prominent art historians, one of whom pressed the point that the Louvre survived the French Revolution and the Kremlin endured the Bolshevik takeover *(see figures 12 and 13)*. For the East German Communists, the Berlin palace loomed not as a worthy landmark but as a hated vestige of Prussian militarism and capitalist rule. "May it no longer remind us of an inglorious past," the official party newspaper *Neues Deutschland* commented just before dynamite ripped apart the facade.[53] It took four months to completely remove the monumental four-story quadrangle of twelve hundred rooms with a dome at one end. Ulbricht dreamt that a skyscraper like the ornate Stalinist towers in Moscow would one day stand in the palace's stead, housing central government organs. For the moment, the palace's terrain was simply renamed Marx-Engels-Platz and inaugurated as a demonstration arena by a million East Germans on May 1, 1951. On that day, the party Politburo assembled on a tribune, much like their Soviet comrades did atop Lenin's Mausoleum, as the masses marched by. Within this framework, the proletariat provided the ultimate architectural ornament. But outside of rallies and parades of military hardware, the area was empty and the destruction of the palace left a gaping void at the heart of the old city.

The void proved difficult to fill. Economic shortages and ideological confusion following the death of Stalin in 1953 led to repeated delays in designing a new power center for East Berlin. Nikita Khrushchev's denunciation of his predecessor's personality cult and erroneous policies entailed criticism of architecture as well, notably the high cost of Stalinist decorative design. "Soviet architecture must be characterized by simplicity, austerity of form, and economy of layout," read a resolution signed by Khrushchev. "Buildings must be given an attractive appearance, not through the use of contrived expensive decorative ornamentation, but by an organic connection between the architectural form of the building and its purpose, between good proportions and a proper use of materials, structures, and detailing, and through high-quality workmanship."[54]

To implement this, the Soviet Union embarked upon the comprehensive industrialization of building operations in 1955. East Germany again followed Moscow's example despite the fact that party propagandists had just recently been energetically condemning modernism while stressing the Germanness of historicist buildings. Kurt Liebknecht, an architect who served on the East German Communist Party Central Committee and was the nephew of socialist hero Karl Liebknecht, signaled that the East Germans were ready to change tack and renounce excessive ornamentation when he cited Khrushchev's remark that there was no need to transform a "modern apartment building...into a church or a museum."[55]

Amid these changes, divided Berlin was becoming a cold-war showcase for competing architectural visions that mirrored the ideological rivalry between the two superpower blocs. In 1957, a diverse group of leading architects including Le Corbusier, Hans Scharoun, Alvar Aalto, and Walter Gropius contributed designs for an international exhibition of architecture called the Interbau and located in the Hansa district of West Berlin. The area's random layout and stylistic pluralism were seen by West German officials as a democratic reply to the pomp and ostentation of the Stalinallee. Chancellor Adenauer wrote in the exhibition catalogue that its design ideas would "radiate both westward and eastward." West Berlin Mayor Otto Suhr put it more directly. "Barely a kilometer away from Interbau there begins the other Berlin, another world, separated from us but still belonging to us," Suhr wrote. "The new buildings, from now on, extend toward that boundary and will prove their powers of attraction."[56] In the same year, the Federal Republic of Germany sponsored an international competition for redesigning Berlin as the eventual capital of a unified Germany. The area treated in the West German competition spanned well into the Soviet-occupied area of the city, a move taken in the East as a clear political provocation.

For their part, the East Germans organized a "Competition for the Socialist Redesign of the Capital Center of the German Democratic Republic," also international in scope, but open only to architects from the East bloc. The competition guidelines called for a government megalith on the Marx-Engels-Platz, fronted by a heroic monument to the two socialist theorists. The structure would function as a secular temple, a cathedral of socialism, a *Stadtkrone*, the city's crowning element and culminating symbol of its identity. To the astonishment of East German authorities, Henselmann submitted a radical proposal for a soaring Television Tower in place of the centralized government structure. It projected a high-tech image topped with a shining red glass sphere containing viewing platforms and a restaurant. Although it had no chance of gaining approval in the prevailing political and aesthetic climate, the design helped solidify the East German trend towards modernism in the post-Stalinist thaw. The tower plan would eventually be revived, but none of the competition entries was built.

In the late 1950s, East German architects presented a series of designs for a new government ensemble on the Marx-Engels-Platz. Moscow frequently served as the prototype. "The architecture of central Berlin should fill the workers with confidence, courage, and enthusiasm," wrote Gerhard Kosel, president of the East German Bauakademie. "It should lift up the inconstant and be a thorn in the side of the enemies of progress." Kosel was among those who designed a government skyscraper for the Marx-Engels-Platz *(see figure 14)*. He later aspired to create the German variant of Lenin's Mausoleum on Red Square by transferring Karl Marx's remains from Highgate Cemetery in London for display in the center of

East Berlin.[57] Another ambitious proposal put forward by the architect Josef Kaiser involved building a clear glass bubble dome 300 feet high and covering most of the square. Kaiser's design echoed the enormous domed Volkshalle proposed by Speer for Hitler's Berlin. Yet it was endowed with an entirely new look in the communist era through the transparency of glass so beloved of West Germany's politicians.

Still nothing was realized. By 1961, East Germany had taken on a more pressing construction project—the building of the Berlin Wall. The one-hundred-mile-long barrier, hastily thrown up in the form of barbed wire and later reinforced by prefabricated concrete slabs and hundreds of watchtowers, was needed to staunch the flood of East German citizens leaving for the West at a rate of 2,000 per day. What the Communist government defended as an "anti-fascist protective rampart" achieved its goal of checking the exodus. But it also proved a substantial drain on resources that might otherwise have been devoted to more illustrious architectural endeavors. Thus the wasteland in the city center where the Royal Palace once stood remained empty, and soon began to embarrass the Communist leadership. So, with the Wall firmly in place along the frontier dividing East and West Berlin, Ulbricht grew intent on building up the inner core of his capital in time for the twentieth anniversary of East Germany's foundation.

The drive to rebuild East Berlin's war-torn heart stemmed in part from the Communists' desire to gain international recognition for the German Democratic Republic. For years the Federal Republic had claimed to be the sole legitimate representative of the German people, and had successfully isolated East Berlin by threatening to cut off diplomatic ties with any country that recognized East Germany. Frustrated, Ulbricht wanted all the more to burnish his country's image by creating an architecturally significant capital city. "A raging passion for power and a raging passion for recognition played a role. There was a desire to send a signal that we are here, we're not going away," said Joachim Näther, chief architect of East Berlin from 1964 to 1973.[58]

With the government strapped for cash, but still yearning for a demonstrative architectural gesture, Henselmann's Television Tower gained new appeal, since it fulfilled much of the symbolic function of a centralized government office tower at a fraction of its cost. Now that the Soviet Union had launched its Sputnik space program, the streamlined spire was reconceived as a means of communicating the technological prowess and modernity of the socialist state. Construction began in 1964. The tower was completed in the 1969 anniversary year, not on Marx-Engels-Platz but slightly to the east of it off Alexanderplatz. Rising nearly 1,200 feet, it was and remains the dominant feature of the Berlin skyline, a bulbous-topped stalk of concrete easily visible from many parts of West Berlin *(see figure 16)*. The approval of its construction and location was, Näther said, "decidedly political. At the time, Ulbricht wanted to have a kind of urban exclamation point. . . . There was an enormous confrontation between East and West. One sought to outdo the other side. The tower was intended as a built signal that here in East Berlin socialism was under way."[59]

A large glass sphere at the tower's pinnacle contains an observatory and communications equipment. But a fluke in the design of the sphere ended up garbling the tower's symbolic message—the glass was arranged in facets that had the unintentional effect of reflecting the image of a giant blazing crucifix in the sky when bright sunshine hit the tower. "This created an unbelievable uproar at the top levels of the party," recalled Kosel, the architect who oversaw the tower's construction. "It was seen as a provocation, an attempt to damage socialism." The West German media gleefully seized on the design gaffe. Despite efforts to modify the glazed sphere, the cruciform reflection could not be eliminated. "I found it amusing myself," Kosel said after the collapse of the Wall when he lived as a pensioner in a spacious Karl-Marx-Allee apartment.[60]

Gradually the area around Marx-Engels-Platz took shape as the East German power center. The Socialist Unity Party's Central Committee had already moved into the former Reichsbank annex just off the square in 1959 after renovating the massive building for its needs. East Germany officially rejected responsibility for the past and the Communists voiced no qualms about taking over one of the largest relics of the Third Reich—and a one-time bastion of capitalism—as their headquarters. As shall be seen in greater detail later, the architecture's political message was considered neutralized once Nazi imagery had been removed from the dour sandstone facade. The building's size and solidity ably filled the party's space and security requirements. Its position, in immediate proximity to the central square but not fronting directly on it, placed the real levers of power—ultimately controlled over a thousand miles to the east in Moscow's Kremlin—physically off center stage.

Ceremonial institutions were given greater prominence on Marx-Engels-Platz itself. From 1962 to 1964, the Staatsratsgebäude (Council of State Building) was erected at the southern end of the square according to a design by Roland Korn and Hans-Erich Bogatzky. It housed the East German government's executive branch behind a boxy modern facade of red granite, sandstone, and glass. The main entrance was placed asymmetrically at the western end of the building, confirming the break with the classically balanced proportions favored in the Stalinist past, and incorporated remains of the baroque portal and balcony of the Royal Palace from which Karl Liebknecht proclaimed, in vain, the free socialist republic of Germany on November 9, 1918 *(see figure 15)*. The Prussian eagle that stood atop the portal was chiseled away and replaced with the gilded dates 1713/1963—the first denoted the portal's creation; the second its implantation in its new setting as a trophy of a vanquished past, displayed for all to see like a stuffed stag's head in a happy hunter's salon. Inside, a grand staircase was arrayed against a towering stained glass window depicting the history of the German workers' movement. The red-carpeted stairway led upwards to formal reception rooms where foreign heads of state were received and ambassadors presented their credentials.

The Staatsratsgebäude was the setting for a belated surge of diplomatic activity when in 1972, as the crowning achievement of Willy

Brandt's *Ostpolitik*, East and West Germany finally established diplomatic relations. Other Western governments followed suit in opening formal ties with East Berlin. Korn, who served as chief architect of the capital from 1973 to 1989, proudly recalled accompanying Indira Gandhi, Fidel Castro, and Pierre Trudeau on official visits to the paneled reception rooms with ceilings over twenty-two feet high. "One wanted to make an impression with this first state building of the young German Democratic Republic," he said of the design.[61]

On the western edge of the square an architectural collective led by Josef Kaiser designed a modern new East German Foreign Ministry, completed in 1967 *(see figure 40)*. Its expansive white pleated facade, similar to another used by Kaiser at a state-owned department store on the Alexanderplatz, comprised repeating vertical panels of white-painted aluminum that the architect said sought to achieve "calm and monumentality."[62] The ministry's construction required demolition of the remains of another Berlin landmark, Schinkel's Bauakademie, the Prussian state architectural school. Many thought the trade-off inequitable, and after communism's collapse the Foreign Ministry was torn down to prepare for reconstructing a replica of the Bauakademie.

At 150 feet, the height of the twelve-story Foreign Ministry was more than double that of Berlin's traditional cornice line, a level to which city builders had previously tended to limit themselves. The excessive volume came in response to express directives from Communist Party officials. In the decade prior to the building's construction, the Soviet Union had made several overtures to Bonn seeking German unification on the condition that West Germany spurn alliance with the West. According to Günter Kunert, a senior architect who worked with Kaiser, party leader Ulbricht harbored hopes that these offers would gain acceptance even after Bonn entered NATO, and thus envisioned a Foreign Ministry that would serve a state far larger than the German Democratic Republic. When Adenauer held out against unification on Soviet terms, the finished building was larger than needed and a third of its space was given over to the Ministry of Higher and Vocational Education. Paul Verner, the Communist Party's first secretary for the city of Berlin, also asked that the building be high enough to conceal the spires of Schinkel's neo-Gothic Friedrichswerdersche Church, located at the rear of the ministry, from the Marx-Engels-Platz and the roadway leading to it from the east.[63]

Kaiser prepared several variations before the final ministry design was selected. Presenting a proposal to Ulbricht in 1963, the architect recalled that "his verdict was that it was a modern, good, and handsome building, but not yet a Foreign Ministry." The party chief then suggested the building be set upon a base and that there be some sort of "central accent point" on the exterior. Kaiser responded by supplying the building with a pedestal and adding a prominent covered driveway to accommodate dignitaries arriving at the ministry's main entrance. "This instructive critique and stimulus presented a difficult challenge, but in the final analysis it decisively advanced the architectural appearance of the project," he wrote later in the official architectural journal.[64] The architect's description of Ulbricht's role can perhaps be seen as both a wish to curry favor with power and a reflection of the degree to which matters of taste and form were determined at the highest levels at this point in East German history.

By the mid 1960s, the East German transition to a modernist style was complete. This was evident in the extension of the Karl-Marx-Allee with prefabricated slabs of concrete known as *Platten*. *Plattenbau*, uniform buildings made of these standardized elements, rapidly blanketed the country and many cities around the Eastern bloc. In Berlin, the application of standardized construction techniques reached a new peak with the rebuilding of Leipziger Strasse, also completed in time for East Germany's twentieth anniversary in 1969. East-West rivalry played a role here as well since Leipziger Strasse ran parallel and in close proximity to a section of the Berlin Wall opposite where West German media magnate Axel Springer had built a tower emblazoned with his logo and electronic news flashes. In response, East Berlin built a series of four apartment blocks each twenty-five stories in height and an office tower thirty stories tall. The erection of the Leipziger Strasse towers, commented *Deutsche Architektur*, demonstrated that "the ideals of the revolutionary battle have found their realization in the socialist German state."[65]

This effusive rhetoric aside, there was a creeping recognition by East German authorities that industrialized building production and standardized design fostered by the state-planned economy was creating a ubiquitously dull urban environment. East Germans began to share the same doubts that arose in the West about the anonymous city centers left in modernism's wake. The Communist Party Politburo in 1968 declared that "bold and original urbanistic and architectural solutions are needed to counteract monotony... in order to give built manifestation of the optimism and strength with which our people create socialism."[66]

The appeal opened the way for the flashiest element on the Marx-Engels-Platz, the Palast der Republik (Palace of the Republic), a project overseen by Erich Honecker, who took over from Ulbricht as party chief in 1971 *(see figure 42)*. Aligned on axis between the Television Tower and the Brandenburg Gate, the building was encased in copper-tinted reflective glass and white marble. Its oblong form equally recalled the Palace of the Soviets in Moscow and the Kennedy Center for the Performing Arts in Washington, D.C. and filled roughly the footprint previously covered by a central courtyard of the Royal Palace leveled in 1950. The design of this people's palace strove for what its chief architect Heinz Graffunder called a "bright, festive elegance,"[67] and it did succeed in bringing unaccustomed glitz to the dreary East Berlin center. The colored facade mirrored sunlight during the day and shone by night from inner illumination, giving the city a new focal point at the eastern terminus of Unter den Linden.

Its interiors were lavish and fanciful; some looked as if created by the American resort designer Morris Lapidus. Decorative elements included myriad chandeliers of dangling glass globes, a black and white marble floor in a swirling psychedelic pattern, and curved banquettes of plush tufted velvet in a series of theme restaurants whose styles ranged from faux neoclassical to rustic baroque. Many of the building's design features were adapted from Western architectural models. Although most East German architects were barred from traveling to the West, Wolf Eisentraut, the architect who designed its large entrance foyer, said he and his colleagues were given access to and "devoured" foreign architectural journals.

"We wanted it to be something special for a person to go into the palace," said Eisentraut. He recalled the ball held to inaugurate the building in 1976 to which construction workers and their spouses were invited along with the Communist Party elite. "As I watched them come in, I observed their faces filled with joy and astonishment. It was clear that we had achieved our aim."[68] Though the building earned the Italianized German epithet of "Palazzo Protzo" (Ostentatious Palace) in West Germany, within the confines of the East bloc the Palace of the Republic set a new standard. Its concept and form were imitated in communist-built halls for Prague, Sofia, and Havana.

The multipurpose Palace of the Republic itself had no equivalent in the Federal Republic. About a third of the building housed the East German parliament, the Volkskammer, or People's Chamber. But the legislature met only a few times a year and its presence inside the palace by no means turned the building into an official preserve like the Foreign Ministry or Staatsratsgebäude at other sides of the Marx-Engels-Platz. On the contrary, the palace was open to all as a state-subsidized national community center. It contained a separate 5,000-seat auditorium for theater and musical performances as well as sporting events. Eleven restaurants, a bierstube, cafes, bars, a bowling alley, and meeting halls made the building a popular place for East Germans to spend leisure hours as well as a choice setting for private celebrations of weddings, graduations, and retirements. Food and drink were available at moderate prices and in a plenitude unknown elsewhere in the country.

Outside, the facade was adorned with the Communist state seal composed of a hammer and compass. Its terrace had a built-in parade tribune for the party leadership to preside over the annual May Day parade.

The reviewing stand was minuscule in relationship to the vast expanse of copper glass behind and it was used only once, in 1976. The following year, the party opted to move the parade and other political marches to the more spacious Karl-Marx-Allee because the addition of the Palace of the Republic to Berlin's central square, now fronted by buildings on three sides, rendered it a difficult space for maneuvering tanks and heavy military hardware.

The monument to Karl Marx and Friedrich Engels envisioned for the Marx-Engels-Platz was never realized there. Instead, the socialist heroes were diverted to a landscaped area at the rear of the Palace of the Republic, after an artistic collective led by Ludwig Engelhardt submitted a subdued sculpture in 1984 that was better suited to a low-key park setting. The work showed Marx seated with Engels standing behind him, an arrangement that led Berliners to tell the following joke: Marx asks, "How much has all this cost?" And Engels responds, "You had better sit down before I tell you."[69]

Even as the quip made the rounds, still more of East Germany's scarce resources were being spent on prestige projects. The emphasis now had shifted from new buildings to restoration of war-damaged areas of the city in time for another anniversary, a date supposed to mark 750 years since Berlin's foundation. By the time that came in 1987, East and West were still vying to outdo one another architecturally. The East Germans concentrated on turning Berlin into a showplace that hid mounting economic shortages elsewhere in the country. Just a short walk from the Marx-Engels monument, great effort went into faithfully reconstructing the Nikolai Quarter, once the heart of the medieval town, as a sightseeing attraction of cobblestone streets lined with pubs, shops, and restaurants that could help draw Western tourists and their much-needed hard currency. The renewed attention to Berlin's historic center also derived from an official reassessment of Prussian culture as a means of legitimizing a separate East German identity in an era of increased contacts with the Federal Republic. Corresponding with the postmodernist architectural trends in the West, East German architects began using precast concrete elements that were no longer just simple slabs but arches, lintels, pillars, and other quotations from architecture of the past—design elements that had been forsworn since the post-Stalinist thaw.

These belated efforts at design innovation could hardly rival the colorful collage of architecture that brought new verve to West Berlin at around this same time. With the 1987 International Building Exhibition, or IBA, a follow-up to the 1957 Interbau, heavyweight architectural ammunition was once again deployed in the western part of the city. Charles Moore, James Stirling, Arata Isozaki, Peter Eisenman, and Paolo Portoghesi were among the architects who took part in IBA, drawing up subsidized public housing projects. Many of the projects were built on bombed-out city blocks dormant since the war's end.

Meanwhile, in East Germany's last decade of existence, Marx-Engels-Platz languished as an unwitting metaphor for the Communist leadership's thwarted aspirations towards a capital of monumentality and splendor. It became an unsightly parking lot for apparatchiks, a sea of East Germany's noisy Trabant and Wartburg automobiles, spewing fumes and clattering as they entered and exited what was once envisioned as a pilgrimage spot for the international proletariat. All around this would-be cathedral of socialism, popular dissatisfaction grew over the reality behind the official architectural facade. In November 1989, the discontent found an outlet in the massive anti-Communist protests that took place on the square and opened the way for yet another government to set its own stamp on Berlin.

DESIGNING NEW IMAGES OF POWER

As late as January 1989, East Germany's Communist leader Erich Honecker was assuredly proclaiming that the Berlin Wall would stand for another hundred years. When it buckled just ten months afterwards and opened the way to German unification in 1990, the Federal Republic's leaders in Bonn were every bit as unprepared as Honecker and his Politburo. The West Germans had long ago resigned themselves to the durability of national division and were busily overseeing the expansion of their seemingly permanent "provisional" capital by constructing Günter Behnisch's new Bundestag along the verdant edge of the Rhine.

Finally called upon to make good their pledge to return to Berlin, many Bundestag members were reluctant to actually leave the cozy town that had suited their purposes so well for forty years. Uprooting themselves and moving the 380 miles eastwards was by no means a matter of course, even if decades of lip service had been paid to doing just that. Berlin's location, as close to the Polish border as Bonn is to the eastern edge of Belgium, provoked worry that Germany would reorient itself away from its NATO allies. Along with these geopolitical concerns, the prospect of giving up the pastoral calm of the Rhineland for the hubbub of a metropolis with a population of 3.5 million made Bonn's advocates fight all the harder. Berlin was also smack in the middle of the daily travails unification entailed. Basing the government there meant returning to the historic epicenter of Nazi atrocities and East German communist oppression. Its war-torn terrain contained far too many minefields for a country acutely aware of the ideological implications of architecture and urban planning.

These reservations found expression in the narrow margin of the Bundestag's 337 to 320 vote, taken on June 20, 1991, to relocate the government seat. Some Bonn residents, anxious that their town would swiftly return to obscurity once the government packed up and moved away, literally hung white flags from their windows. Many Bonn-based civil servants, however, were not yet ready to surrender. They used foot-dragging to draw out the move's time-table and complicate its terms.

In an attempt to appease these opponents, the government decided that, for the foreseeable future at least, it would not leave town en masse. The Chancellery, the Parliament, and ten key ministries would relocate, while eight ministries would stay put and establish secondary offices in Berlin. In another concession that added complexity and crisscross confusion, several smaller federal agencies previously based in Berlin would be transferred westward to Bonn. The 1991 vote resulted in not only a welter of logistical and organizational planning but also heated discussion about the appropriate architecture for a revitalized Berlin.

Already by 1991, the ideological triumph of capitalism over East bloc communism was taking its most prominent built form with plans for new corporate office towers for Daimler-Benz and Sony on the reborn Potsdamer Platz. The location of the former East-West border crossing Checkpoint Charlie underwent transformation into a business center sponsored by a consortium of u.s.-based investors. Amid the construction commotion at these and dozens of other private-sector projects that turned the city into Europe's largest building site, the unified German state grappled with its own architectural reconception.

The splendid centers of most European capitals were ordered up by powerful leaders, but Germany had for much of its history held design competitions for major public buildings. Unified Berlin's official center was reinvented through such contests judged by government officials, urban planners, and architects. In a demonstration of German openness, leading foreign architects were invited to both award and vie for prizes. So many celebrated names from around the world took part that some competitions resembled the architectural equivalents of the G-7 summit. Jury deliberations were often the scene of stormy debate, particularly between foreign jurors and the Germans themselves.

The first and most significant contest was for a master plan for the capital's main government district, a concept that the Germans had long avoided in Bonn. Called the International Urban Design Idea Competition for the Spreebogen—the Spreebogen was a site that encompassed and took its name from an arc-like bend in the River Spree immediately northwest of the former imperial parliament, the Reichstag—it entailed not specific buildings but an overall scheme to determine the layout and location of key state institutions. Since the construction of the Wall near the Spreebogen in 1961, this area had been relegated to the periphery of the divided city, but it found itself at the very center following unification.

Architects from as far afield as Tel Aviv, Tokyo, and Tallinn presented their own visions about how Germany should rebuild the political apex of its capital. In all, 835 proposals were received from 44 countries. Hundreds of West German architects submitted designs. By contrast, only a handful of East German architects took part in the 1992 competition. By that date, the generations of architects who had played an instrumental role in designing the Communist capital had begun dying off or gone into retirement, and the survivors who managed to readapt for architectural practice under changed political and economic circumstances felt the deck was stacked against them. "We had no chance," said Günter Stahn, designer of the Nikolai Quarter in East Berlin, among the few East Germans who entered the competition.[70] Unification, the East Germans learned, effectively involved the consensual annexation of East Germany by the Federal Republic. Their political and economic institutions were replaced almost overnight by West German ones. The changeover and the introduction of capitalist methods left all but the youngest and most professionally agile East German architects struggling to keep pace. The new Berlin would be planned largely on Western terms.

Joining the German government officials represented on the jury were several foreign architects, including New York-based Richard Meier and Karen Van Lengen, both of whom had designed projects in Germany. Ironically it was the foreign participants who pressed most insistently for an overall scheme that was reflective of united Germany's status as Europe's economic powerhouse. Bonn politicians gravitated towards a decentralized antiurban design recalling their provisional capital's muted arrangement. The preference was not simply a matter of taste or habit; they were nervous about a clear embodiment of state power. "They wanted to say, 'We're just this little country in Europe,'" Van Lengen said. "They're very sensitive about it because they know the world is watching them."[71]

Unification did prompt foreign leaders and the proverbial man in the street to ask whether the enlarged Federal Republic, which was previously so content to be an economic giant but a political dwarf, might turn into another kind of titan or even a bully. Around the same time as the Spreebogen competition, a seminar of experts briefing British Prime Minister Margaret Thatcher for a visit by Chancellor Kohl drew up a list of German characteristics that included aggressiveness, complacency, and ruthlessness. Thatcher herself feared a unified Germany could become a "bull in a china shop" and fretted that France was rushing headlong into a European federation as "a way of tying down Gulliver" within a supranational structure.[72] Unfettered by the tact required of a responsible politician, the American comedian Jay Leno told "Tonight Show" viewers, "I'm sure that you have heard that Germany has been reunited. The only question now, I guess, is when it will go on tour again."[73] That sort of wisecrack heightened Germans' awareness that half a century after World War II their actions were dogged by their dark past.

The past weighed especially heavily on the Spreebogen selection process since the 150-acre site is the very same tract where Albert Speer envisioned the vast north-south axis, framed at opposite ends by a huge domed Volkshalle and a gargantuan victory arch *(see figures 17 and 18)*.

Even though Speer's plan actually mimicked the route of a 1917 proposal by Martin Mächler calling for a new boulevard to intersect a republican Berlin, the north-south axis promoted under the precarious interwar democracy was too tainted by association with Nazism to permit its use by unified Germany. Speer's ghost haunted the jury deliberations, so only schemes with an east-west axis were seriously considered by German members of the jury. Many of the foreign jurors found the German historical sensitivities superfluous and outmoded. During two weeks of heated deliberations, the French architect Claude Vasconi accused the Germans of cowardice and fear of architecture itself. "Symbolism in architecture need not be synonymous with the Third Reich. It's not everyday that one has the chance to rebuild a capital," he said. "One should make the most of it and not be afraid."[74]

Still the Germans remained ever watchful of signs of grandeur better left in check. Politicians who would have preferred to retain the government seat in Bonn kept their distance from any architecture that might indicate that the Berlin-based republic would amount to anything other than the Bonn-based Federal Republic writ large. Their concern about this was manifest throughout the review of the Spreebogen submissions. Frequently, Van Lengen said, government officials looked to the foreign jurors for their reaction to this or that competition entry, asking whether its design contained unwanted political signals. "What are we saying to the world? That we're going to take over the world again?" she was asked.[75]

Ultimately, the foreign architects swayed the deliberations and jurors settled on a proposal for a new hub of German power designed by Berlin architect Axel Schultes, terming it a "bold representation of the democratic state."[76] The Schultes plan, designed with his colleague Charlotte Frank, called for creating an east-west corridor of federal buildings over half a mile long and reminiscent of the Mall in Washington, D.C. *(see figure 19)*. Known as the Band des Bundes or the Federal Strip, the corridor seemed modest in comparison with the U.S. capital. Nonetheless, it involved a degree of architectural muscle-flexing that would have been off limits in Bonn. Even after it was chosen, many Bonn officials continued to be put off by the corridor's daring form that thrust itself across the river bend. They read authoritarian connotations into it and pressed for its reconsideration.

The clearly delineated design reflected Schultes's insistence that Bonn's random placement of government structures was inappropriate for the unified capital. Transferring this "cows in the pasture" layout to Berlin, he said, would "be the end and not the beginning of a new, a different period of representation of the German state."[77] There could have been no greater contrast to Bonn than what he proposed: a massive ribbon of federal offices twice crossing over the Spree, knitting together the eastern and western parts of the once-divided city as it cancels out Speer's north-south axis. The corridor sought to make unification manifest in the urban landscape, extending from the Moabit section in the west of the city, across an area previously traversed by the Berlin Wall, and into the Friedrichstadt district in the east. The plan functions as a gigantic girder or truss repairing the fissures of a metropolis torn asunder by decades of East-West conflict. Running just north of the Reichstag, the corridor is as wide as a football field, with the Chancellery and its gardens at the western end and offices and a library for the Bundestag at the other. "The challenge posed by the competition was to coax the soul out of the Spreebogen, the genius loci, to pour its historical and spatial dimensions into the mold of a new architectural allegory," Schultes said.[78]

Publicly acknowledging the skepticism of Bonn politicians, Schultes drew on his considerable oratorical skills to reassure them. Any monumentality, he stressed, would be softened by a break he inserted at the corridor's midpoint, where he proposed that the government build a public place of assembly that he called the Civic Forum. Schultes said he wanted the forum to be accessible around the clock to all citizens. He further urged that it become "a place of civil courage" and an area where individuals "can heal themselves of the malady of being German."[79] Such an arena was certainly different from anything the Nazi or the Communist regimes envisioned for their capital city Berlin. Or was it? It was perhaps symptomatic of the supposed ailment itself that a state-commissioned architect felt the need to create an officially sanctioned training area for the exercise of democracy. Gerhart Laage, the Hamburg architect who served as jury chairman, predicted that the assertive form of the Federal Strip would become the equivalent of a new corporate logo for Germany. But soon after its selection he voiced concern that national decision makers could "lose courage" to fully carry through with its implementation.[80] The remark proved prescient.

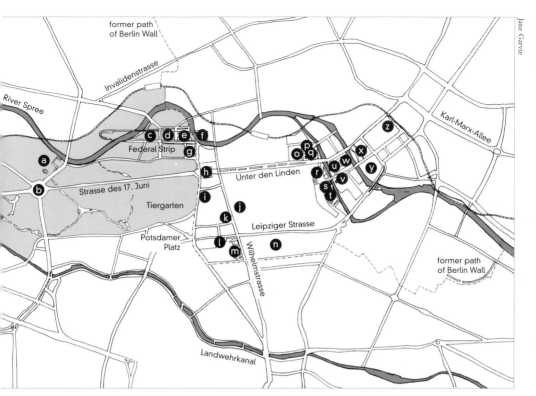

1   Map of Berlin with locations of projects discussed.

a Schloss Bellevue and Presidential Office
b Prussian Victory Column
c Chancellery
d Civic Forum
e Parliamentary Offices
f Parliamentary Library
g Bundestag (former Reichstag)
h Brandenburg Gate
i Proposed site of Memorial to the Murdered Jews of Europe
j Ministry of Labor (former Propaganda Ministry)
k Former site of Hitler's Reich Chancellery
l Bundesrat (former Prussian House of Lords)
m Finance Ministry (former Aviation Ministry)

n Former site of Checkpoint Charlie
o Neue Wache
p Addition to German Historical Museum
q German Historical Museum (former Prussian Arsenal)
r Former site of Bauakademie and East German Foreign Ministry
s Foreign Ministry addition
t Foreign Ministry (former Reichsbank)
u Schlossplatz (former Marx-Engels-Platz)
v Council of State Building
w Palace of the Republic
x Marx-Engels Monument
y Nikolai Quarter
z Television Tower

2 Pädagogische Akademie—former teacher's college designed by Martin Witte and converted into the West German Bundestag in Bonn. Its Bauhaus style, reviled by the Nazis, was viewed by post-war German leaders as a sign of their desire for a new start.

3 Political transparency in architecture—spectators peer through glass windows to follow proceedings of the West German parliament's inaugural session from bleachers erected outside the Bundestag in Bonn, September 7, 1949.

4 Embassy of the Federal Republic of Germany in Washington, D.C., soon after its completion in 1964. Designed by Egon Eiermann, the humanely proportioned diplomatic mission was a billboard image for a German state seeking to demonstrate that it had changed its ways.

5 Kanzlerbungalow in Bonn, completed in 1964 and designed by Sep Ruf. The modest residence projected an air of quiet distinction and style for the postwar West German government chief.

6   Bundestag office tower in Bonn, nicknamed "Tall Eugen," a Teutonic "Big Ben," with the original
    Bundestag Building at far right. John le Carré termed Bonn "discreetly temporary in deference to
    the dream" of returning to Berlin, but "discreetly permanent in deference to the reality."

7   West German Chancellery in Bonn, completed in 1976, with a statue by Henry Moore in the
    forecourt. The Moore was chosen after Chancellor Willy Brandt vetoed plans for a globelike statue
    for fear the work might be misinterpreted as a sign of renewed German international aspirations.

8 Bundestag in Bonn designed by Günter Behnisch and completed in 1992. Its entry facade has been likened by critics to an airport hall or train station. The architect wanted a building that would remind politicians that not they, but German voters, are sovereign.

9 The Bundestag's circular plenary chamber designed by Günter Behnisch to avoid traces of hierarchy. The light-filled chamber was intended to project an open and friendly character.

10 Stalinallee in East Berlin, built in a neoclassical style that, according to the Communists, reclaimed
for the proletariat architecture that was previously the preserve of the aristocracy and
the bourgeoisie.

11 Stalinallee, looking towards a pair of twin towers known as Frankfurter Tor. "The time is gone forever when a privileged few lived in palaces, while shoebox-like structures of spittle and ash were
deemed good enough for the workers," proclaimed an East Berlin magazine.

12 Hohenzollern Royal Palace in Berlin, a quadrangle of 1,200 rooms built over centuries and destroyed by the Communists in 1950 to make way for mass demonstrations.

13 Destruction of the former Royal Palace in Berlin begins on orders of the Communist government in September 1950. "May it no longer remind us of an inglorious past," declared the official Communist Party newspaper.

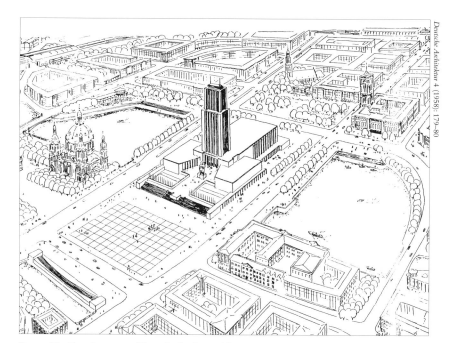

14 Proposal by East German architect Gerhard Kosel for a central government building on the site of the former Royal Palace (never realized). The new structure was to function as a secular temple, a cathedral of socialism.

15 East German Council of State Building, completed in 1964 and incorporating remains of the Royal Palace in its entryway. In its new setting the palace portal was displayed like the trophy of a vanquished past.

16 East German Television Tower, completed in 1969—an urban exclamation point that the Communists viewed as proclaiming the technological prowess and modernity of the socialist state.

17 Albert Speer's proposed north-south axis (never realized). The soaring domed hall in the background was to have been the centerpiece of "Germania," a Berlin transformed into a capital worthy of Hitler's Thousand-Year Reich.

18 Proposed Volkshalle designed by Albert Speer for Nazi Berlin to accommodate up to 180,000 people (never realized). Its cavernous interior would have been so large that Speer worried about clouds forming under the domed ceiling.

19 Federal Strip designed by Axel Schultes and Charlotte Frank, the winning entry in postunification Berlin's Spreebogen competition. The design knits together eastern and western parts of the once-divided Berlin as it cancels out Speer's planned north-south axis.

20 Hitler's Reich Chancellery designed by Albert Speer. Its facade comprised square fluted pillars, deep-set windows, and an eagle grasping a wreathed swastika in its talons. Hitler stressed that "when one enters...one should have the feeling that one is visiting the master of the world."

21 The Reich Chancellery, completed in 1939, was over a quarter mile long. A political scientist noted that the building "speaks volumes about the imperious nature of the Nazi state and the megalomania of its head."

22 German Ambassador's Residence in Washington, D.C., designed by Oswald Mathias Ungers. Completed in 1994, it was criticized as a "monumental declaration of power" that embodies "precisely what Germany does not wish to be."

23 Proposed Federal Chancellery by Krüger-Schuberth-Vandreike, which provoked concern over what some saw as its likeness to Speer's designs for Nazi Berlin. "As an expression of a pluralistic, democratic polity, this work is simply unacceptable," protested a leading journal.

24 Competition-winning proposal for Federal Chancellery by Axel Schultes and Charlotte Frank, with oculi in the facade. These were later modified after Berlin Mayor Eberhard Diepgen dubbed them the "eyes of the chancellor."

25 Interim proposal for Federal Chancellery by Axel Schultes and Charlotte Frank, using a treelike facade to embody the merging of East and West Germany. Schultes later discarded this proposal, calling the imagery "naïve."

26 Final design of Federal Chancellery for unified Berlin by Axel Schultes and Charlotte Frank. Schultes wanted a design that "does not look like a so-called fat Germany" but that would instead elicit "sympathy at the first glance."

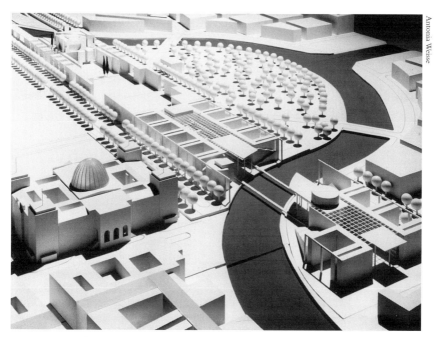

27 Eastern portion of Federal Strip for unified Berlin. In the foreground are the Bundestag Library and Offices designed by Stefan Braunfels (right) and the Reichstag (left).

28 Competition-winning plan of the Presidential Office by Martin Gruber and Helmut Kleine-Kraneburg. The office ellipse is at left and the President's Residence in Schloss Bellevue is the U-shaped building at right.

29 The design of the Presidential Office, a black granite ellipse, was rejected by President Roman Herzog as "unfriendly."

30 Revised design for Presidential Office with larger windows for greater "transparency" and a lighter stone that may help avert a monolith of gloom from arising in the capital of post-Auschwitz Germany.

Schultes's master plan left the architecture of individual buildings to be determined by subsequent competitions. A key component of his Federal Strip was the headquarters of the first chancellor to govern from Berlin since Hitler. In December 1994, another jury deliberated over its design. Again, the specter of Speer lurked in the minds of German politicians on the panel. Although Speer's marble-lined Chancellery was destroyed on orders of the Soviet army after Berlin's conquest in World War II, the image of this notorious building lived on as the epitome of what they sought to avoid at all costs.

After taking power in 1933, Hitler rejected the Chancellery he inherited as inadequate, saying it looked "like the headquarters of a soap-box company, not the center of a Reich."[81] Speer's replacement, built at breakneck speed to be occupied in less than a year and completed in 1939, aimed to correct the earlier Chancellery's shortcomings by intimidating everyone in its vicinity *(see figures 20 and 21)*. The building was over a quarter mile long. Its facade comprised square fluted pillars, deep-set windows, and an eagle grasping a wreathed swastika in its talons. Hitler stressed that "when one enters the Reich Chancellery, one should have the feeling that one is visiting the master of the world."[82] Foreign dignitaries and other callers entered through massive bronze gates to a court of honor two hundred and forty feet long. To reach Hitler's offices, they ascended a flight of stairs and progressed through a series of richly decorated reception rooms before reaching a gallery four hundred and eighty feet long, twice the expanse of the Hall of Mirrors at the Palace of Versailles. Even this was insufficient to satisfy Hitler's craving for splendor. He had Speer draw up an even larger Führer Palace for the Spreebogen. War impeded its completion, although subterranean foundations were laid and these had to be demolished in 1993 when unified Germany began clearing the site for its own state architecture.

Bonn's nondescript Chancellery arose as a visceral repudiation of Speer's designs, but failed to express any coherent new vision about the democratic state that succeeded Nazi Germany. Chancellor Helmut Kohl saw a need for a clearer architectural statement in Berlin, but was uncertain about exactly what that should be. Aides said he sought a reasonable built expression of a democratic leader's power, turning the volume neither too high nor too low. "There's certainly no desire for great gestures," said Chancellery Director General Hans-Achim Roll.[83]

German anxiety about any contemporary parallels with the Nazi past strew a number of pitfalls in the way of selecting a Chancellery design. As in the Spreebogen competition, an officially sponsored jury included a range of German and foreign architects, with representatives of Kohl's office having had a minority vote. The Chancellery competition was open to architects from throughout Europe. Over 250 architectural offices applied to participate. Of these, 51 were asked to submit designs. Sifting through the entries, jurors again focused on questions of symbolism. One design in particular raised concerns about its mighty horseshoe-like plan, reminiscent of a Roman theater and encased within colonnades that entirely sealed it off from the proposed Civic Forum. The closed horseshoe was an archetypal form that inspired the never completed Congress Hall, drawn up in 1934 by Ludwig Ruff for the Nazi party's rally grounds at Nuremberg.

The author of this disputed Chancellery design was Oswald Mathias Ungers, a Cologne-based architect whose scheme for the German Ambassador's Residence in Washington, D.C. had recently ruffled more than a few feathers (see figure 22). The austere columned building in the U.S. capital was commissioned by the West German government prior to unification, and since completion in September 1994, it has been portrayed in Germany as an egregious diplomatic blunder. The first envoy to live there, Ambassador Immo Stabreit, openly decried its "ice cold atmosphere."[84] Chancellor Willy Brandt's former speech writer, Klaus Harpprecht, called it a "monumental declaration of power" that embodied "precisely what Germany does not wish to be."[85] The residence, where the ambassador receives and entertains some 9,000 guests annually, sits on a hill adjacent to the 1964 embassy designed by Egon Eiermann. Whereas Eiermann's design sought to show a Germany that was unobtrusive and humane, Ungers's building reflected a stiff and uncompromising nature. The *Washington Post* said it occupied the hilltop site with the "authority of an aesthetic field marshal."[86] Germany's most prestigious newspaper, the *Frankfurter Allgemeine Zeitung*, assailed the Spartan interior for having the "antiseptic charm of an intensive care unit."[87] The critiques were not wide of the mark. Many jurors saw the same worrisome characteristics in Ungers's proposed Chancellery, and some regarded it too as making an inappropriate expression of a "claim to power" on Germany's behalf.[88] The Ungers design did garner enough support to earn it third place, while drawing vehement opposition from those who blocked it from taking the top competition slot.

The jurors were unable to settle on a single winner and instead awarded two first prizes from forty-one entries. They left the final decision, passing it on like a hot potato, to Kohl himself. The two top choices were polar opposites that magnified the symbolic architectural quandary facing the government. One was an abstractly modern structure drawn up by Axel Schultes, who had won the Spreebogen masterplan competition. The other first prize went to another highly formal colonnaded palace designed by a young East German team, Krüger-Schuberth-Vandreike, whose members had graduated from architecture school just before the demise of the Communist state *(see figure 23)*. Their proposal reminded many Germans of the very demons that Behnisch and his contemporaries sought to exorcise for decades in Bonn. It unleashed a storm of indignation.

"As an expression of a pluralistic, democratic polity, this work is simply unacceptable," the architectural journal *Bauwelt* said of the plan.[89] The weekly journal *Die Zeit* assailed its "feudal air" and worried that Germans had an "atavistic" impulse towards monumentality.[90] Peter Conradi, the Social Democratic parliamentarian who delights in playing the role of gadfly in official architectural matters, was so incensed that he photocopied Krüger-Schuberth-Vandreike's elevational drawings and paired them with Speer's for the Führer Palace. He was not the first to make the fatal connection, but he went furthest in actively seeking to torpedo the proposal by circulating these copies around Bonn.

Thomas Jefferson may have deemed classical forms to be ideally suited to the expression of American democracy, but in the Federal Republic of Germany these same forms often bring out a response that is almost phobic. "In Germany, classicism by virtue of having been requisitioned by Hitler is simply impossible to use again," said Conradi. His own aversion ran so deep that he made an analogy to the phrase "*Arbeit Macht Frei*" (Freedom Through Labor), which was emblazoned over the entry to the death camp in Auschwitz. "No one can say that anymore," he went on. "Actually it's a very nice phrase, an accurate phrase. It could well be the motto of a social democratic party. But the vocabulary is finished. One can no longer use it."[91]

A new generation of German architects rejected his argumentation. It was incomprehensible to architect Torsten Krüger, then thirty-one years old, who saw no good reason why he should be barred from tapping into Berlin's own tradition of classicism as envisaged by the nineteenth-century Prussian architect Karl Friedrich Schinkel. "This taboo is a form of political correctness," Krüger said, accusing Conradi of vilification. Krüger clearly felt the need for a new architectural dignity in Berlin, terming Bonn's buildings "self-castigating." Talking of his team's vision for the new Chancellery, he said, "It doesn't signal that Germany is again falling prey to totalitarianism. Rather, this building has an imperturbability and calm that one needs in order to be a good partner."[92] But he struck some Germans as recklessly indifferent to the burdens of their history when he dismissively recalled how his architectural professor in the former East Germany, much like the West German Behnisch, heard military marching as soon as he saw a design with more than three columns in a row. "That is his life experience, not mine," said Krüger. "We have another biography."[93]

The dichotomy between the two Chancellery proposals, and the clash of ideas between Krüger and Conradi, raises the question of whether specific architectural forms—be they Speer's Doric columns, Schwippert's glass walls, or Schultes's east-west axis—express ideological content. A conviction that they do guided Bonn's development and design for forty years. This was understandable in light of the German experience: the Nazis suppressed Bauhaus modernism, rejecting the social goals of its exponents and thereby marking an end to a period of "liberal chaos." Designs inspired by Greek and Roman antiquity were used instead to signal a return of security and order to the Reich. The Nazi repudiation of materials like glass and steel heightened their democratic and progressive image in postwar Germany; neoclassical buildings of stone were seen as inherently totalitarian.

The same controversy surfaced in a battle sparked around the same time by the Berlin city government's architectural guidelines for private development in the unified capital. Implemented by Hans Stimman, municipal building director from 1991 to 1996, these sought to ensure the preservation of a local architectural tradition by requiring masonry facades that followed traditional height limitations and street patterns. The art historian Heinrich Klotz saw in this a revival of Nazi-era architecture and warned that Berlin was on the road to becoming a capital where Hitler would feel at home, a place he called "New Teutonia." Sounding the alarm in a much-discussed interview, Klotz declared, "For God's sake, not this kind of capital!"[94] The deconstructivist architect Daniel Libeskind talked darkly of "authoritarian and repressive edicts" and an "ugly atmosphere that resembles the pathology of a time when the notion of degenerate art was born."[95] Taking the opposite view, Vittorio Magnago Lampugnani, former director of the German Architectural

Museum in Frankfurt, denounced the automatic defamation of architects as fascist once they opt to build in traditional styles and solid materials like stone and wood. "Perhaps this is the nemesis of German architecture: It is barred from the entirety of its own tradition as punishment for the terror that it represented and cosmeticized in the thirties and forties."[96]

To Lampugnani's dismay, many Germans continue to equate classical forms with Nazi symbolism. When the British architect James Stirling unveiled his winning proposal for Stuttgart's Neue Staatsgalerie in 1977, a building that became an emblem of postmodernism, Behnisch accused him of having fascist tendencies because the design involved stone facades and quotations from the classical past. Behnisch viewed Stirling's design as inhuman and overly monumental for a free and democratic society. Nearly two decades later, discussing plans for the move to Berlin, Behnisch again argued that the German government could not build in a classical style for fear that it could awaken reactionary tendencies. "They could become virulent again," he said, maintaining that the use of classical forms should be declared "out of season" or off-limits for many years to come in Germany. "It's much too dangerous to take them out again. They would summon reactions in a multitude of directions."[97]

Berliners had a chance to judge the two very different Chancellery proposals for themselves at an exhibition in January and February of 1995. Comments written in the guest book included calls for "greater courage!" to create a new monumentality. Other visitors were repelled by the Krüger-Schuberth-Vandreike plan, regarding its chilly Palladianism as a dangerous omen. One likened it to a prison; another apparently saw it as unduly martial, and wrote, "We have put Prussia behind us." When the models were shown in a national television report about the controversy in March, the ARD network asked viewers to phone in their preference. Over 33,000 callers or 79 percent voted for the colonnaded arrangement, against more than 9,000 or 21 percent backing Schultes's design.[98]

Kohl was long thought to share the popular preference for the grander and more readily comprehended Krüger-Schuberth-Vandreike design. It held an additional allure for him in that its architects hailed from the former East Germany. Awarding the important commission to this young team would have been an easy means of scoring political points for a chancellor frequently accused of riding rough-shod over easterners' sense of self-worth. But in the weeks leading up to his decision, many critics and other commentators began a campaign to steer him in the other direction.

Like most laymen, the chancellor has difficulty reading architectural drawings. To facilitate his understanding of the choice foisted upon him, the state body overseeing the project, the Federal Building Board, created large-scale models of both designs. Each covered a surface the size of a Ping-Pong table and was kept in Kohl's Bonn offices for six weeks. Still he could not make up his mind. Displaying the caution that helped him become the longest-serving German chancellor since Bismarck, he summoned seventeen prominent figures to provide counsel. In a sign of concern about foreign reaction, the group included not just architecture specialists but a leading expert in diplomatic history and the Third Reich, Klaus Hildebrand, along with Goethe Institut President Hilmar Hoffmann, who backs an intensive policy of cultural diplomacy to overcome what he has termed ongoing foreign resentment towards Germany.

Kohl and this group of advisors met in Bonn to weigh which of the two designs best fulfilled the functional requirements of the chancellor and his 400-member staff as well as provided the optimal setting for weekly government cabinet meetings. Symbolism was another major preoccupation at the closed-door colloquium where the competing architects were asked to explain their design's expression of the German res publica. After hearing the responses, the panel unanimously urged Kohl to go with the modernist scheme by Schultes, both because of the perceived superior quality of his work and the manner in which it projected the national identity. The chancellor took their advice. Stressing the need for "a dignified architectural environment that would shape the image of our state beyond our borders," Kohl announced on June 28,

1995 that he chose Schultes since he had produced a design that "radiates confidence, modesty, and dignity" and looks to the twenty-first century.[99]

It would be an exaggeration to compare Axel Schultes's role with that of Schinkel in embellishing Berlin for King Friedrich Wilhelm III, let alone with Speer's under the Third Reich. But more than any other contemporary architect Schultes has indelibly marked the official district of the once-and-future capital by virtue of having provided its master plan and the Chancellery design that fits into it. "As a colleague I can understand Speer very well," the silver-tongued Schultes said after winning both competitions. "It's a seduction for an architect to sit in the lap of power." Wrestling with that temptation, he struggled to formulate a new architectural image for the German government in unified Berlin, something that he hoped would become "the icon of the move."[100]

While Speer's Chancellery for Hitler sought above all to intimidate and overawe, Schultes wanted the design he drew up for Helmut Kohl to elicit "sympathy at the first glance."[101] Here was a goal for architecture that was unusual in the history of capital planning. In East Berlin, Communist architects had talked of creating buildings that would inspire confidence, courage, and enthusiasm. In Berlin unified under a liberal democratic order, the chancellor's architect desperately wanted his work to win public approval. Although Schultes was alone among his colleagues in so explicitly articulating this aim, it stemmed from a widespread German impulse that surfaced repeatedly as officials planned the new Berlin. The bid to inspire sympathy—and at the first glance—highlighted the degree to which Germans felt compelled to reassure the world and themselves that they had renounced aggrandizing and predatory behavior once and for all.

Schultes agonized over the commission, describing it as "burdened with all that the Reich Chancellery once was, what was envisioned for this place and so on. It is not easy." He said that with the Federal Republic's Chancellery he was seeking "to correctly gauge the power of its statement, so that it is not pompous, so that it does not look like a so-called fat Germany.... There is the difficulty of creating something that is fitting, but that makes clear that this is not a corporate headquarters, that it's not a labor union building, rather that this is where the government sits." Thus Schultes's architecture made a clear break with Bonn's anonymous, low-key approach and avoidance of symbolism. "This is no longer understatement," he said. "We are moving forward and we have to respond. It's no longer possible to duck the issue." With the government buildings in Berlin, he said, the "republic must show its colors."[102]

Just what these colors were remained unclear. Was German democracy as practiced in the 1990s a concept well enough understood in the popular mind to permit communication in architectural form? Of course, the Federal Republic was a solid democracy very different from any state authority previously based in Berlin. It was deeply anchored in liberal Western values like parliamentarism, free speech, and an independent judiciary. It also had emerged as the most powerful force within Europe, but Germany was as yet undecided about how to exercise its might within the European Union, other than seeking to ensure fiscal rigor in order to preserve its own prosperity and the strength of the German mark and its proposed successor, the single European currency unit, the euro. In these circumstances, was modern architecture, or Schultes himself, up to his self-described task of symbolizing the body politic?

Schultes is a soft-spoken fifty-four-year-old who peers out from behind half-moon glasses. His sole major building prior to the Chancellery was the Bonn Art Museum. It was completed in 1992 just across the Adenauerallee from Kohl's Bonn offices. Some Germans use the term "archaic-modernist" to describe its style, since in the manner of Louis Kahn it manages to combine twentieth-century materials like glass and smooth concrete with the mystical grandeur of the temples of Karnak or Hagia Sofia. Schultes cites both ancient Egyptian and Byzantine architecture as inspiration for his work.

Seeking fresh sources for Berlin, Schultes studied two acclaimed modernist capitals, Le Corbusier's design for Chandigarh, the state government complex in Punjab, India, and Kahn's political citadel for Dhaka, Bangladesh. Schultes won Kohl's support with a Chancellery proposal that had large oculi cut out of its facade *(see figure 24)*. Kahn had used a similar motif in Dhaka. But when computer-generated drawings were published in the summer of 1995, some officials felt the perforations might translate badly, bringing an unwelcome iconography of "Big Brother" to the former hometown of the Stasi and the Gestapo. As soon as Berlin Mayor Eberhard Diepgen dubbed them the "eyes of the chancellor," Schultes scurried to devise a less fraught image. The architect reshaped the circular openings on the north and south facades of the building so that they resembled half ovals, blunting the ominous connotations that worried the mayor.

A nine-story cube housing the government chief's executive offices and cabinet meeting rooms forms the core of the Chancellery and is flanked by two lower five-story wings for Chancellery staff. The mass of these wings, filling the outer edge of the Federal Strip, is lightened by a series of glass-walled gardens. Schultes originally wanted the Chancellery to be of a single, uniform height, but Kohl requested him to double the size of the core so that his office would not be fully outflanked by the nearby Reichstag. The revised balance will more accurately reflect the constitutional relation between the executive and legislative branches.

After winning the Chancellery competition, Schultes devoted a year and a half to revising and fine-tuning the eastern facade, which will include the main entry to the building. Since this will serve as a media backdrop when official pronouncements are made and foreign statesmen come calling, it requires a telegenic presence that gives it instant recognition at home and abroad, something that the Bonn Chancellery failed miserably to achieve. The distinctive architecture Schultes devised stands head and shoulders above the Bonn Chancellery, successfully striking a note of neither pomp nor false humility.

Having reshaped the round openings into ovals on the building's sides, he toyed with the idea of an entry facade that took the unusual form of a split tree trunk, roots, and branches. This derived from former Chancellor Willy Brandt's declaration after German unification, "What belongs together, must grow together" *(see figure 25)*. Schultes tested the public response to the treelike facade by presenting it at a news conference in June 1996. He displayed a blue Styrofoam model of how this arboreal imagery might look in poured concrete, and readily conceded that the built product could verge on kitsch. Yet he obviously felt a once-in-a-lifetime commission like the Berlin Chancellery compelled him to experiment in new directions. "We need to borrow very plastic, very simple expressions to create an impression that one cannot achieve with normal bare-bones architecture of walls, columns, and windows. Here one needs something more. Architecture has limited possibilities to release feelings. Architecture can always communicate a feeling of lightness or weight. It can be elegant, it can be ugly, threatening, ponderous, but to arouse a feeling of sympathy is another matter."[103] After several months of further experimentation, Schultes discarded the tree, saying he realized that its imagery was "naïve" and "in the long run that it would wear thin."[104]

Schultes also considered a spare, colonnaded portico with a pair of high entry doors. The prospect of using tall columns at the Berlin Chancellery set off alarm bells in Kohl's office after the uproar surrounding the Krüger-Schuberth-Vandreike design and the perception that it had Speerian echoes. Kohl himself was said to be personally uncomfortable with the imagery. In the final design unveiled in February 1997, Schultes avoided using any sort of conventional columns. Instead, he devised a series of rippling panels of formed concrete forty-six feet high *(see figure 26)*. "It's a dimension with which one does have to be on guard," Schultes said. "One certainly cannot deal with them in a carefree way." Behind these panels, the main facade was no simple glass box, but a play of contrasts between sheets of glass and walls of concrete and natural stone. In symbolic terms, the contrasts are a truer representation of the political process than found in an ostensibly transparent glass house like the Kanzlerbungalow or the Behnisch Parliament in Bonn, where pretensions to actual democratic monitoring of interior activity via the facade are specious. "Here there is a suggestion of openness," Schultes stated. "It's only a feeling of openness. Unfortunately, it's not the real thing. No one gets in there."[105] The facade gives passersby a view inside while the forecourt actually bars entry.

Making the building appear approachable rather than forbidding and aloof was paramount in planning the ceremonial court that fronts the main facade and is bounded by the wings of the Chancellery. In this area, formally called the Cour d'Honneur, Germany's leaders will roll out the red carpet for state visitors. Schultes had intensive discussions with Chancellery aides about the court's composition; they knew that if the proportions were not just right Berlin could again end up with pretentious corridors of power like those Charlie Chaplin parodied in *The Great Dictator*. Schultes was not to create a hermetic precinct where world leaders come and go undetected. Instead he was expressly instructed by Kohl to further the image of government openness by ensuring that the arrival of state guests would be visible to citizens gathered at the Civic Forum.

Additional factors influencing the Chancellery's appearance were the designs for the Bundestag Offices and Library at the opposite end of the Federal Strip. These were the work of a great admirer of Schultes, the Munich architect Stefan Braunfels, who was awarded his commission in yet another competition in October 1994. Braunfels's proposal won over the judges of that contest in large part for its success in diluting the strip's monolithic feel. He averted the erection of forbidding, fortresslike walls, but faithfully kept the outline of Schultes's corridor through a lighter structure of glass and concrete arrayed in a comblike pattern around landscaped courtyards *(see figure 27)*. His design has more in common with the tradition of public building in Bonn than what has previously been erected in Berlin. The Bundestag Offices' glass entry under a large and welcoming overhanging roof faces the Civic Forum. An inner atrium is surrounded by offices and eighteen parliamentary committee rooms. The leitmotif of transparency is culminated in the upper-level visitors' gallery that tops each committee room and that enables public observation of the proceedings. In Bonn committee sessions were held behind closed doors. But in Berlin German parliamentarians, who had studied the functioning of u.s. congressional committees in Washington while drawing up plans for the move, would open up their meetings to the public.

Two foot bridges—one for the public and the other reserved for parliamentarians—link Braunfels's office complex on the west side of the River Spree with his rotunda-centered Bundestag Library on the opposite, eastern bank. The silhouettes of the bridges attempt to carry the Federal Strip's outline across the river. But these forms, sketchy in contrast to the buildings they link, make it evident that Schultes's competition-winning master plan has a greater architectural clarity on paper than in reality. Its ribbonlike appearance on a map, intended to symbolize the merging of East and West Germany, will be experienced very differently from a pedestrian's vantage point—not as a single unified bar but as a fragmentary urban element that falls short of expectations in repairing the fractured relationship between the city's parts.

Increasing the lack of architectural cohesion, the centerpiece of the corridor, the Civic Forum, has been placed on hold for the time being. The forum site will be publicly accessible, but without any architectural component as foreseen in Schultes's master plan. Instead, at its very heart, the Federal Strip will have to rely on a provisional landscaping arrangement, including lawns and allées of trees, four deep along each side, to maintain its sweeping outline until the day when German politicians are prepared to build the forum. The failure to realize this essential central element of Schultes's plan reveals the German government's suspicion of a truly public realm. Perhaps no German politician was eager to have a built-in focal point for protest in immediate proximity to both the Parliament and Chancellor's Office.

The length of the strip itself has also been considerably diminished. The strip was originally to extend well into the Friedrichstadt section of eastern Berlin, but now will halt abruptly short of there after making its eastward thrust across the Spree in the form of the Bundestag Library. The reason for the truncation was partly financial. In 1994, Kohl justified spending on more assertive government building than had been seen in Bonn. "The federal capital of Berlin is attaining an exceptional role in the cultural image of Germany," he told parliament. "Our federal capital must live up to what is expected of it. Our responsibility... for the move of the parliament and parts of the government to Berlin involves not only questions of architecture and organization. We also must ensure that the character of our polity as the freest state in German history will be clearly visible in Berlin."[106]

But by the time construction of the Federal Strip had begun in 1997, the Finance Ministry was increasingly desperate to comply with criteria for participation in the European Union's plan for a common currency. Restructuring the bankrupt East German economy, involving annual transfers of tens of billions of marks from West to East, soaked up far more money than Kohl's government projected. This complicated its struggle to keep the federal budget deficit below three percent of gross domestic product, the standard that Germany itself had set for participation in the European monetary union. Facing these fiscal constraints, Germany could ill afford overly extravagant expenditures on capital architecture for fear of angering both its European partners and its own taxpayers, who bore the brunt of cuts in social benefits to plug the deficit. In addition, by early 1997 German unemployment was running a postwar record of 12.2 percent, and Kohl was obliged to abandon an ambitious plan to cut taxes when he faced an uphill battle for reelection in September 1998.

The ever-present fear of parallels with Berlin's Nazi past had another impact on the masterplan, since extending the strip into the Friedrichstadt would have required demolishing residential buildings, including a Communist-era apartment block commissioned in East Berlin just before the fall of the Wall. The prospect of some 160 tenants protesting against their forced eviction to make way for the new state architecture raised unwelcome historical echoes. Under Speer's direction, vast areas of Berlin, including parts of the Spreebogen, were forcibly cleared and over 50,000 apartments were torn down.

The postponement of the Civic Forum and the failure to extend the Federal Strip eastwards considerably undermined Schultes's symbolic intent of inscribing unification into the Berlin urban landscape. Now its fragmented, unbalanced form will reflect the ongoing inequality of wealth between East and West. It will have a far grander western end with the Chancellery and its riverbank gardens, but sputter out with a shabby eastern terminus where the strip halts at the prefabricated brick- and concrete-paneled apartment complex. The watering down of Schultes's design typifies the implementation of capital city planning in a modern democracy like Germany, where not only the architect, but a pluralistic client with conflicting ambitions, political agendas, and aesthetic tastes, shapes what ultimately gets built. "Our concept was born in the euphoria of unification," Schultes said with some resignation. "The jury said that the concept's great expanse was to be implemented. Previously we believed that the federal government would simply have more power at its disposal in Berlin, but since so many people rejected the concept from the very beginning, a lot of sand got into the gears."[107]

PRESIDENTIAL OFFICE
GLITTERING JEWEL OR DARK FORTRESS?

When Roman Herzog succeeded Richard von Weizsäcker as German president on July 1, 1994, he stepped into the shoes of a man who had enjoyed considerable esteem at home and abroad. The German president, a largely ceremonial head of state with little actual power, concerns himself in part with educating the citizenry about democratic values and setting an appropriate moral tone for the nation. During his term, Weizsäcker cogently warned against letting Nazi atrocities slip out of memory. In his inaugural speech as reunified Germany's first president, Herzog, former chief justice on the country's highest court, immediately addressed the weighty issue of the national past, saying that it still burdened the Federal Republic's relationships with its neighbors. Many of these, he noted, regarded the enlarged German state with great suspicion.

While expressing the wish that Germans "must become more sure of ourselves than we are at present," and insisting that "the love of our country should not be silenced for a moment," Herzog urged that citizens of reunited Germany "take pains to use a decidedly soft tone. National hullabaloo, fanfare, and the clashing of cymbals are the last thing that we need."[108] The admonition also applied to the president's attitude to the rebuilding of Berlin. Thus Herzog found himself in an awkward spot when he learned about the proposed design for a new Presidential Office, the Neubau des Bundespräsidialamtes, to house his administrative staff, chosen just weeks before he took office in one of the government-sponsored architectural competitions.

The design, by Martin Gruber and Helmut Kleine-Kraneburg, a young Frankfurt-based duo in their early thirties, called for an elliptical black granite structure *(see figure 28)*. Enthusiasts called it jewel-like, a cabochon to be set in a wooded park adjacent to the presidential residence in Schloss Bellevue, the eighteenth-century palace of Prussia's Prince August Ferdinand. But others, including Herzog, feared that the project resembled a shadowy coliseum, a fortress, or a massive sarcophagus that risked setting precisely the wrong tone for the German head of state. There were even suggestions from within the Union of German Architects that the president renounce the elliptical architectural plan altogether and quietly hold another competition to come up with a less ponderous design. "We could only shake our heads," the union's dismayed president, Andreas Gottlieb Hempel, said of the stone-faced ellipse. "It gives the impression that the public servants who work inside are bearers of state secrets."[109]

In contrast to the hallmarks of transparency, accessibility, and humanity invoked for decades in Bonn by Behnisch and others, Gruber and Kleine-Kraneburg used watchwords like stability, calm, and timelessness to describe their black house. "Now that one has the chance to build a new capital, it would be a shame not to express a certain confidence," said Kleine-Kraneburg.[110] His partner made their dark design sound like a willful aesthetic provocation to challenge the design credo that prevailed in Bonn. "This is a breaking away from all the unfortunate constraints that have arisen...away from constraints imposed on the architectural discussion, including this fictitious concept of democratic architecture," Gruber said.[111]

The young team discouraged any intimation that the elliptical shape was inspired by the Oval Office in Washington. But like the u.s. president's working quarters, the new Berlin presidential project bears a resemblance to the abstract geometrical simplicity of eighteenth-century French neoclassical architects like Claude-Nicolas Ledoux and Étienne-Louis Boullée. Its sculptural form will stand as a solitary object in the park adjacent to Schloss Bellevue, fitting neatly into its greenery. During the Enlightenment such a form was seen to be based upon a belief in order, reason, and harmony—a reflection of natural law and republican ideals, rather than political absolutism. In postwar Germany, "classicism has always had a negative reactionary tinge," protested Gruber. "In no way is that the case."

The oval Presidential Office, set between the palace and the nearby Victory Column designed to celebrate nineteenth-century Prussian military conquests, would never have been proposed for unassuming Bonn. Undeniably elegant and distinctive, its original design had a detached and enigmatic air that a democratically elected president of a country with a totalitarian past could easily forego. But Herzog was disinclined to make waves in the early days of his term by taking the controversial step of autocratically scuttling the government-sponsored jury's choice. He opted instead to order alterations in the design after meeting with the architects at his Bonn offices in November 1994.

"He said straight away, 'I am responsible for this. I am the one who will be associated with this. . . . It is too forbidding and not the way to represent ourselves to the outside.'" Kleine-Kraneburg recalled, adding with undisguised annoyance, "Such a discussion could take place only in Germany."[112] The president went on to tell Gruber and Kleine-Kraneburg that their four-story design made an "unfriendly impression" and ordered the 240 narrow windows encircling the ellipse enlarged for more "transparency." The young duo begrudgingly complied, nearly doubling the windows in size, but balked at the presidential request that they change the black granite that clad the ellipse to a lighter stone to soften its image *(see figures 29 and 30).*

The jury that chose the design, by a vote of seven to four, had already voiced its own reservations about the use of the highly polished black granite—a stone infelicitously named *Nero assoluto.* By a subsequent vote of ten to one, the jury requested that the architects rework the plan, forgoing stone for a more modest material like unglazed brick for the building's facade. The architects refused to budge on this aspect of their proposal, insisting that their desire for a shiny black granite was purely an aesthetic choice with no symbolic component. The dark facade, they explained, was intended to mirror the surrounding vegetation and allow the building to merge with the landscape.

All the same, black gave the ellipse the stench of death, a funereal aura of doom that was highly problematic for the capital of post-Auschwitz Germany. This unlucky architectural symbolism did not occur to the architects—or if it did, it failed to deter them. Walter Karschies, the presidential aide in charge of administering the project, detected a waning of the sensitivities that had marked the older generation of German political figures. "I notice in my dealings with the architects that they are sometimes totally astonished by my logic and the scruples that we carry around with us," said Karschies. "I am a bit older and this life has left its mark upon us. We have a very fruitful dialogue. Sometimes with regard to architectural questions they devise a solution that seems self evident and I say, 'Watch out, there's this or that sore spot.'"[113]

The adjacent, creamy white, neoclassical, U-shaped Schloss Bellevue has a more welcoming form. Its main facade features four Corinthian pilasters and a modest templelike gable. Two side wings form the edge of a large forecourt and seem to throw open the building in an inviting gesture suited to its current use as the president's permanent base. The palace has had a variety of tenants since its completion in 1787. It became an exhibition space in the 1920s, and under the Nazis served for a while as a Museum of German Ethnology. After 1938, its interior was redesigned as the Third Reich's official guest house. Allied air raids badly damaged the building in 1944, but it was remodeled in the 1950s to become the Berlin residence of the Bonn-based West German president, a symbol of his own commitment to return to the historic capital. After unification, locating the presidency's permanent quarters at Schloss Bellevue dovetailed nicely with the topography of the new Berlin's official power center, since the palace is just west of the Federal Strip.

Despite the warnings by Karschies and President Herzog himself, the architects resisted further changes in their ellipse. Seeking outside help as Chancellor Kohl had done when facing his own impasse over the Chancellery design, Herzog referred the matter of the building's facade to a three-man commission of architects, consisting of two Germans, Otto Meitinger and Helge Pitz, and a Spaniard, Victor Lopez Cotelo. This team reported back that the somber stone was "not acceptable, and also not the appropriate manifestation for a new building of the Federal Presidency."[114] The three consultants then examined a palette of fifteen other shades of stone, and recommended a far lighter green-gray granite that would better enable the building to blend in with its surroundings.

Reluctantly, Gruber and Kleine-Kraneburg went along with the commission's recommendation, having no choice but to do so or lose the coveted job. Several months later, to the architects' delight, the approved green-gray granite turned out to be unavailable in the quantity required. The commission, in turn, suggested using a gray South African stone it judged equally adequate to avert a situation whereby an introverted black house overshadows the more welcoming Schloss Bellevue as the architectural emblem of the German presidency.

The changes seem to have satisfied President Herzog, who publicly at least has made his peace with the architects and their design. Lest the unusual Presidential Office retain any lingering dark connotations or mystery, the presidency set up a large informational panel outside the high wrought iron gates surrounding the head of state's compound while the building was under construction. Affixed to the panel was a box filled with leaflets describing the building's design. In the six-page brochure, Germany took the remarkable step of distributing to the general public detailed blueprints of the official building's layout. "We want to create the impression that we have nothing to hide," said Karschies.[115] At the groundbreaking ceremony on March 14, 1996, Herzog expressed a tentative hope that the structure would be rapidly accepted by Berliners. "There are enough boring buildings!" he proclaimed. "Therefore we have settled on an unmistakable yet unobtrusive building. Perhaps the Berliners will take a bit of capital city pride in it. That would make me happy."[116]

The elliptical object in a sylvan setting will hardly be boring. The substantial enlargement of its windows and subtle modification in the color of its facade may help in transforming the look and feel of what would otherwise have been an impenetrable monolith shrouded in gloom. Yet as the building neared completion, some Germans could not help but worry that Gruber and Kleine-Kraneburg's design had recast an important part of the symbolic image carefully cultivated by the Federal Republic prior to the move to Berlin. For them, the unmistakable Presidential Office still had an elusive, sepulchral quality they regarded as ill advised for the titular leader of a nation that wanted its intentions to be crystal clear.

BURDENSOME LEGACIES

Berlin's largest surviving Nazi-era buildings, the former Reichsbank and Aviation Ministry, are prime examples of the Third Reich's efforts to deploy monumental architecture as a propaganda tool and use huge public construction projects as a means of job creation and economic revival in the 1930s *(see figure 31)*. "Our opponents will come to realize it, but above all our followers must know it: our buildings are built with the aim of strengthening...authority," Hitler declared.[117] The buildings' dark past, some Germans in the 1990s believed, disqualified them from housing the public entities of a democratic capital. Unified Germany would do better to construct new ministries from scratch, ostensibly free of historical burdens.

Soon after the vote to move the government seat, the Bonn authorities envisioned taking a wrecker's ball to the Nazi structures. Building Minister Irmgard Schwaetzer and other Bonn leaders were intent on bulldozing remnants of the defunct East German government as well, such as its Council of State Building, its Foreign Ministry, and its Palace of the Republic. Once these were cleared away, a string of up-to-date ministry buildings would arise on the vacated land.

Dieter Hoffmann-Axthelm, an influential Berlin urban planner and architectural critic, stated that it would be wrong for the government to "heedlessly" reoccupy buildings that had served the criminal Nazi regime and "cover up the [original] function with an apparent neutrality."[118] Their reuse by today's Germany was highly questionable. He proposed that they be handed over for occupation by international tenants like the United Nations or the Conference on Security and Cooperation in Europe.

The call for eliminating the tainted historic architecture, made by Schwaetzer in late 1992 and provisionally approved by the federal cabinet a few weeks later, relied on an architectural consultant's report that found the structures unsuitable for use as modern offices. But in a city that had witnessed repeated destruction of its historic buildings, the plan alarmed the local Berlin government and mobilized a substantial conservation lobby that spanned a political spectrum from conservative to progressive. The city government, in turn, commissioned another consultants' report that determined that tearing down the structures and rebuilding new ones of the same size would be more expensive than renovating them. The report also deemed the Reichsbank, the Aviation Ministry, and the Council of State Building to be "landmarks of the first rank," equally deserving of preservation. "There are alternatives more appropriate to the culture of Berlin and the Federal Republic of Germany than simply disposing of history by tearing down buildings," the report concluded.[119] In any case, it warned that the heavy stone Nazi-era buildings would not be easy to eliminate. The destruction of the Reichsbank alone would take at least a year to accomplish.[120]

This was not the first move towards sweeping Nazi remains under the carpet. In the period immediately following World War II, some key Nazi structures were regarded as too politically toxic to leave standing. The Soviets flattened Hitler's office, the Reich Chancellery designed by Albert Speer, and used the scrap marble to build a subway station and Berlin memorials to Moscow's fallen soldiers. United States General Dwight D. Eisenhower ordered the destruction of the Hellenic-style temples built in Munich by Hitler to enshrine Nazism's "martyrs" in the birthplace of the movement. But countless other Nazi-era buildings were left largely untouched. Any ethical misgivings about reusing them fell by the wayside amid a critical shortage of intact infrastructure. A cursory architectural variant of de-Nazification—the removal of swastikas and Nazi inscriptions—was deemed sufficient to render them "disinfected," neutral shells in the popular consciousness. In many cases, little or no effort was made to recall the buildings' origins. Hitler's grandiose Nazi Party Headquarters, where the Munich Accord was signed, became a state music academy in which students perfected partitas unaware of the previous occupant. The House of German Art in Munich remained in use as an exhibition hall, forfeiting part of its name to become simply the House of Art. Barracks erected for the Third Reich's Wehrmacht were taken over by armies of the two Germanys and the four victorious allies. The parade grounds built for Nazi Party congresses in Nuremberg underwent a more banal transformation; they became the scene of high-speed auto races and rock concerts.

Such pragmatism eventually prevailed in unified Berlin. As plans for moving the capital progressed, an economic recession set in and government officials were faced with the staggeringly high cost of German unification. By late 1994, financial constraints together with opposition to razing functional buildings pushed the government to roll back considerably its call for eliminating Berlin's difficult architectural legacies. Chancellor Kohl replaced Building Minister Schwaetzer with Klaus Töpfer, who took a more realistic approach to reusing older buildings in East Berlin that became federal government property upon unification. He decided that ninety percent of the federal bureaucracy would be housed in the buildings already in hand, calling it a form of environmental "recycling" that would be welcomed by the citizenry.[121] The government also placed an overall limit of 20 billion marks, or roughly 12 billion dollars, on expenditures for its move to Berlin, including all capital reconstruction plans. This meant that aside from the new Presidential Office, the fragmented Federal Strip in the Spreebogen, and the new Chancellery and Parliamentary Offices, all ministries would be housed in renovated structures.

The decision to reuse old buildings rather than erecting new ones left cabinet ministers to jostle among themselves in something like a game of musical chairs to determine which federal agency would take over which historic structure and its associated symbolic burdens. The Finance Ministry, the primary advocate of holding down costs of the capital transfer, agreed to take up headquarters in Hermann Göring's massive

Aviation Ministry from which the Luftwaffe waged its terrifying air war to conquer Europe. The Labor Ministry had to make do with the former Nazi Ministry of Popular Enlightenment and Propaganda, from which Joseph Goebbels put German culture into a totalitarian straitjacket and directed his anti-Semitic diatribes in press, radio, and film.

Unified Germany's decision to reuse these buildings did not imply support for fascist policies. But as its partners in the European Union were worried about renewed dominance of the continent from Berlin, German government officials were concerned that a return to these megaliths might heighten simmering suspicions and resentments. In symbolic terms, what could be more awkward than the Foreign Ministry setting up shop inside the imposing former Reichsbank, a building whose architectural design was personally selected by Hitler and which after the war served for thirty years as headquarters of the East German Communist Party? Not surprisingly, Foreign Minister Klaus Kinkel fought vigorously against government pressures for him to accept such premises as his new headquarters. An internal ministry newsletter distributed to diplomats in 1992 explained that Kinkel desired an architectural setting that "did justice to the ministry's special concerns of political image in representing the Federal Republic of Germany abroad.... Future-oriented quarters for the Foreign Ministry in Berlin therefore require a new building."[122]

Kinkel and/or his successors will nonetheless have to execute their daily duties from within the doubly burdened Berlin building long identified with both Nazi and communist repression. Elsewhere in the world, other governments have adapted buildings of fallen rulers for their own use. Russian President Boris Yeltsin occupies the tsarist-built Kremlin where Lenin, Stalin, and other Communist leaders reigned. Sir Edwin Lutyens's palace for the British viceroy in New Delhi has become home to independent India's democracy, and Mexico's president governs from the sixteenth-century Spanish palace erected by Hernán Cortés. The retention and reuse of these structures helps endow today's rulers with an air of authority and stability, and over time the buildings have acquired new symbolic significance. Will time and new occupants ever erase the stigma associated with Berlin's buildings?

So far, the Foreign Ministry is doing its best to put a positive spin on its new location. "I think it's not at all bad for the federal government to constantly be conscious of living and working against the backdrop of a difficult history," said Fritjof von Nordenskjöld, the Foreign Ministry official overseeing its move to Berlin.[123] "These buildings will leave their mark on the policies that are made there," said Andreas Nachama, a Berlin historian who has avidly fought against the eradication of the Third Reich's unholy remains. "Every civil servant who works there, every minister, every state secretary, every representative who comes in and goes out will be aware of them."[124]

The natural tendency of postwar German authorities to seek out positive aspects of the past on which they can base a future will color that awareness of the buildings' infamous history.[125] A selective appropriation of German history is already influencing the official interpretation of the democratic government's reoccupation of the Berlin buildings. "We can occupy this building very easily," said senior Finance Ministry official Hans-Michael Meyer-Sebastian as he sat in the Aviation Ministry where the bombings of Coventry, Rotterdam, and Guernica were planned. "It was a building of the resistance during the Third Reich."[126] Meyer-Sebastian was referring to the Red Orchestra resistance group, which operated covertly within the Luftwaffe Headquarters until the arrest and execution of its leading members. As the building underwent renovation in 1997, the lobby contained a small exhibition paying tribute to the Red Orchestra's courage. There was no marker on the facade—aside from the powerful architecture itself—alluding to the building's genesis or documenting the military aggression plotted there. A plaque affixed four years after the collapse of the Berlin Wall recalled only the anti-Communist demonstration held in the forecourt at the start of the 1953 workers' uprising crushed by Soviet tanks.

Will this stress on the more appealing legacy of resistance activities obscure Germans' understanding of the buildings' broader context and distort the role they played in validating totalitarian rule? "The buildings cannot be seen in isolation," said Winfried Nerdinger, an architectural historian who is director of Munich's Architecture Museum. "They stand in a direct connection with the military industry and often with the concentration camps. I have always objected when people say, 'Oh, these are merely neoclassical buildings. They are harmless, innocent stones that one can deal with today.' They remain bloodily entangled and one must see them in their entirety or do injustice to history."[127]

The Reichsbank exemplifies this legacy of bloody entanglement. It was the first prestige architectural project to get under way after the Nazis came to power. A competition for the central bank building, actually an addition to the nineteenth-century Reichsbank Headquarters next door, was held in the weeks following Hitler's appointment as chancellor in January 1933. At this point, the Third Reich's architectural credo had not yet been firmly determined. The competition guidelines set out the symbolic importance of the commission, stressing that the contest came in the midst of Nazism's rise and at a moment "in which the art of construction must also announce its goals." That the new design needed to impress was also emphasized. "An expansion of the state bank is unthinkable as merely a rational office building. It must have the character of a monument, it should be an ornament for the state capital and should represent the dignity of a world institution."[128]

Mies van der Rohe, Hans Poelzig, and Walter Gropius were among those who submitted designs. But a jury of experts was unable to choose a winner from six finalists, among them Mies with a striking modernist proposal. In the meantime, Reichsbank President Hans Luther had been resisting Hitler's requests to provide larger sums for publicly funded employment projects. Hitler had him replaced by Hjalmar Schacht, a nationalist who would prove, at least for a few years, more amenable to financing a German revival. The Führer's involvement in policy and personnel at the state bank drew his attention to its architectural stalemate. Hitler reviewed the proposed designs, but found all of them lacking in grandeur and overly similar to ordinary office buildings. He then personally chose a design that had been prepared prior to the competition by an in-house architect, Heinrich Wolff, manager of the bank's construction department.[129]

Ten thousand people, including brown-shirted storm troopers and members of Nazi organizations from throughout Germany, attended the 1934 laying of the foundation stone for Wolff's design. Hitler presided over the ceremony at the building site, swastika-bedecked and transformed into a lavish stage that was part of the Nazis' effort to depict a national resurgence *(see figure 32)*. The crowd shouted "Heil!" and thrust its arms forward to salute the Führer as he stood before a model of the new bank building, which Schacht called "an example of patriotic will."[130] Construction of the Reichsbank, its modern steel frame skeleton encased in sandstone, lasted six years. The finished product was an enormous labyrinth of spare classicism with nearly one thousand rooms arrayed along seemingly endless corridors *(see figure 33)*. A row of stolid pillars stretched across the main facade, decorated with a large frieze of muscled figures carved by Josef Thorak, whose sculptures also adorned the Reich Chancellery and the 1936 Berlin Olympic Stadium. Swastikas decorated the heavy doorknobs and huge reliefs of bellicose eagles were inscribed on either side of the main foyer walls. At the top of the entry staircase, Thorak placed two pedestals on which he planned to set massive busts of Hitler and the Prussian monarch the Führer revered, Frederick the Great.

The busts were never completed. For by the time the building went into full operation in 1940, Germany was at war. Soon the "final solution" was well under way. The bank's financial functions were augmented by a new and urgent task—stockpiling stolen goods, which arrived in a steady stream from the extermination camps. The newly constructed three-level subterranean vault rapidly overflowed with booty including gold yanked from Jews' teeth, watches, earrings, bracelets, necklaces, rings, and spectacle frames. There were also great hordes of diamonds, silverware, and banknotes seized from Nazism's victims.[131] The identical fireproof region in the bowels of the former Reichsbank was later used to safeguard the Communist Party's top-secret documents. After 1999, the same vault will store the Foreign Ministry archives.

Andreas Marx, an architectural historian advising the government on the Reichsbank's latest conversion, pressed the government to openly acknowledge the building's history. At a meeting with government officials soon after the 1994 decision to reuse the former bank as the Foreign Ministry, Marx said, "Mr. Töpfer expressed the view that Hjalmar Schacht had given some very critical speeches . . . [in] an attempt to argue that the Reichsbank was simply a banking institution and that Hjalmar Schacht was an obstructionist" to Nazi rule.[132] Although Schacht did join the small resistance movement to Hitler in the last years of the war, Marx objected to Töpfer's summation and pointed out Schacht's key role in putting Nazi Germany on a war footing. "No single man in all of Germany would be more helpful to Hitler in building up the economic strength of the Third Reich and in furthering its rearmament for the Second World War than Schacht," William L. Shirer wrote of the Reichsbank president in *The Rise and Fall of the Third Reich*.[133] Hitler replaced Schacht with Walther Funk as Reichsbank chief in 1939, and the bank became increasingly enmeshed in officially sanctioned brutality. Nuremberg war crimes trial testimony showed that the bank was well aware of the source of its unusual "deposits." Funk was sentenced at Nuremberg to life imprisonment; Schacht was acquitted.

"One should portray the [building's] history as it is," Marx said. "There's no sense in lying and afterwards having the Israeli Foreign Minister visit and then learn from some media campaign about all the things that happened there. It's better to lay it all on the table and discuss it."[134] After Marx emphasized this point, the Foreign Ministry agreed to have him and architect Peter Kroos author an official publication about the Reichsbank for distribution to visitors. "We will see how far we can, should, and must go into details" of the building's history under both

Nazi and Communist regimes, ministry official von Nordenskjöld said. "It is important for the people who work here to know what happened before them within these walls." The desire to inform has its limits, however. Von Nordenskjöld said that the Foreign Ministry has no plans to affix any sort of plaque on the building itself to document its history. "We don't need it. The building speaks for itself." [135]

The structure's history and architecture were bound to create public relations anxiety for the government. "I was concerned that the image of this building would always appear on television when state visitors arrived," said Barbara Jakubeit, the former Federal Building Board President. "In Europe everyone can tell that it belongs to that era." [136]

The Foreign Ministry's need for additional space pointed the way to resolving this symbolic quandary with architectural sleight of hand. Despite its enormous size, the Reichsbank was insufficient to house all 2,500 members of the ministry's capital-based personnel. So Jakubeit organized a government-sponsored design competition for an extension. The guidelines stated that the facade of the old building "will be hidden from the public eye" by the new addition covering an entire city block in front of the Reichsbank. "The new building will have a powerful impact of its own," the competition brief added, underscoring that the Foreign Ministry's "architectural identity will be determined by the new structure." [137] Just how to carry out this gesture, equal to having a construction crew paper over an unpleasant reminder, was left up to competition entrants.

In December 1995, sixty architectural offices were selected to participate, and half a year later the jury chose a design by the Berlin-based Swiss architect Max Dudler. His submission involved not a single structure but two seven-story cubes, one for the ministry's library and the other for the administrative offices. A gap between them allowed a partial view of the Reichsbank from the front of the ministry extension. But with its regimented pattern of identical square windows, the overall effect was as monotonous and dour as the facade of the Reichsbank it was intended to obscure. The critical reception was decidedly unenthusiastic—*Der Spiegel* likened it to "a fortress with openings for gun barrels."[138] Dudler's design, Jakubeit said, was "incapable of making a statement about our age, about our totally different democratic identity."[139] In August 1996, the Foreign Ministry disregarded the decision of the jury—an option it had reserved for itself under the terms of the competition—and gave the commission to the second-prize winners, the Berlin architects Thomas Müller and Ivan Reimann.

Their proposal, featuring a large glass atrium or loggia, posed a greater contrast to the old building and, in the ministry's eyes, made a more convincing gesture of democratic renewal. Müller and Reimann housed the offices and the ministerial library under one roof, thereby fully blocking the view towards the Nazi-era building from the front. But rather than having the new structure directly abut the old and cover it up entirely, the architects left a narrow courtyard between their extension and the former Reichsbank, where the foreign minister's office will be located. The court will serve as a ceremonial space for the arrival of visiting diplomats and foreign ministers of other nations, who will clearly detect the ghosts of the German past in the historic portion of the ministry just opposite the architecture of the new annex *(see figure 34)*.

The atrium at the front of the annex will serve as the general public's main entry to the Foreign Ministry. Five stories in height, it will provide expansive views of Karl Friedrich Schinkel's neo-Gothic Friedrichswerdersche Church and the proposed site for the reconstruction of his Bauakademie. The architects aimed to create a building that did not shut itself off from the rest of the city, like most government structures, but by means of the atrium was integrated with its surroundings. They envisioned the atrium as a space accessible to the general public as if it were an enclosed park with benches and a cafe. "One can drink a cup of coffee and feel part of this whole, while inside ambassadors take part in negotiations," said Müller.[140]

How accessible the new building will be in actuality depends on security requirements imposed by the ministry. Even before these were finally determined, the ministry portrayed the light-filled annex as embodying its current self-understanding. "We are no longer the agency of secret diplomacy," said von Nordenskjöld. "We are a service enterprise that pursues the interests of Germany and its citizens abroad: economic, touristic, cultural. We are a modern agency that engages in dialogue with the public. If one does not make one's foreign policy intelligible to the public, then it won't be supported by the public. This modern annex should mirror this thinking as far as possible."[141]

As part of their proposal, Müller and Reimann submitted a perspectival drawing of the atrium that was cleverly evocative of a famed 1829 sketch with which Schinkel documented the brilliant spatial arrangements at his nearby Berlin Altes Museum (see figure 35). The drawing itself must have gone some way to garner support for their plan, which does not fully merit comparison to Schinkel. Even if it does represent an improvement over the design by Dudler and contrasts with the Nazi-era Reichsbank, the Müller-Reimann scheme seems unlikely to provide a memorable image for modern Germany's involvement in world affairs.

For the renovation of the Reichsbank itself, the Foreign Ministry chose the Berlin architect Hans Kollhoff, who proposed infusing the somber stony labyrinth with natural light, natural greenery and color. These elements could be highly effective as keys towards unlocking the building for reuse in a new age, but because of Kollhoff's own architectural approach, his modifications will probably accentuate the building's inherent severity. Kollhoff is known for his rigidly geometrical architecture not dissimilar from the stripped classicism of Heinrich Wolff's Reichsbank. "This is a very solid building, one has the feeling that it could stand for centuries," he said, voicing unabashed admiration for a design that bears some resemblance to 1930s architecture erected in Washington, Moscow, or Rome. "Despite its rather conservative, gloomy style, this building's structure has a whole series of technical and architectural refinements that one encounters over time and realizes that much of this gloominess, particularly in the interior, is due to postwar renovations." Kollhoff aimed at a renovation that would not "degrade or stigmatize the essential structure that we have from the Reichsbank or from the East German era as something antiquated, unusable, or wrong. We are respecting it for the first time; we accept it as an essential part of a historical layer, but we are adding to it anew."[142]

Major modifications to the building were first undertaken after 1949 when it was used as the East German Finance Ministry, and after 1959 when it was occupied by the Central Committee of the Socialist Unity Party of Germany, the East German communists. Kollhoff is attempting to eliminate those elements that altered the positive qualities of the original design. He hopes to bring in more natural light by opening up windows and skylights sealed during earlier renovations, and to use landscaping to alleviate claustrophobic views onto the drab interior courtyards. The office formerly occupied by Communist Party leader Erich Honecker will be torn down, and roughly the same space will be occupied by Foreign Minister Kinkel and/or his successors. "Erich's fortress will become an open building—for Berliners and for our partners around the world," Kinkel said as the renovations began in 1996.[143] The offices of party Politburo members on the same floor will also be gutted to make way for new spaces to accommodate the Foreign Ministry state secretaries, comparable to U.S. assistant secretaries of state.

Intervention by landmark preservation authorities led to the retention of several other parts of the building, including the Politburo meeting room, with its forty heavy chairs upholstered in a plush red fabric and arranged around a U-shaped conference table. But the architects clashed with preservationists over whether to keep the pillars on which Thorak's busts of Hitler and Frederick the Great were to rest as well as a ceiling painting dating from the Nazi period that was uncovered during the renovation. Kollhoff eventually got his way in having the pillars removed and the painting rendered invisible with a neutral interim ceiling, as it had been under the Communists. "In a building where state visitors are to be received this would be too strong a reminder," said Tobias Amme, Kollhoff's project director for the Reichsbank refurbishment.[144]

A strong palette of colors is being added to walls, floors, and ceilings by the artist Gerhard Merz, whom Kollhoff asked to help with the interior design scheme to give the solemn building a new freshness and visual unity. To some, Merz was a thorny choice because of his coy use of fascist symbols in art installations over the past decade. Hans-Ernst Mittig, a Berlin historian specializing in fascist-era architecture, opposed his involvement since he regarded the artist's installations as calling into question Germany's postwar anti-fascist partisanship. "Works like those of Merz perpetuate, elevate, and certify the practice of superficial and indecisive discourse about National Socialism," Mittig has written.[145] In addition to this contentious political aspect of his art, Merz's aesthetics seemed likely to reinforce the building's chilly atmosphere. Members of the Federal Government Art Advisory Board, reviewing Merz's proposed alterations, expressed particular concern about his plan for the imposing main entrance staircase and foyer. This involved installing a cobalt blue ceiling ringed at the cornice line by fluorescent lights and retaining the original floor of highly polished red porphyry, a combination that some board members feared would create an uncomfortable space in which to greet foreign dignitaries and put them at ease about the new Germany. "One might ask if it would not make more sense to commission artists who would attempt a more critical confrontation with the building," said Art Advisory Board chairman Klaus Bussmann. "Merz has a severity that could be misunderstood."[146]

Like Merz, Kollhoff himself has been accused of pursuing a rightist agenda through a penchant for fascist design, a charge he rejects as confusing aesthetics with politics.[147] "Everything that has a stone facade and a large door is regarded here, in this paranoid situation, as a fascist building," he said. He wants the contemporary visitor to the Foreign Ministry to "always be discovering new constellations. One will only gradually notice what actually belongs to the original Reichsbank building, what derives from the East German era, and what is new. This could have certain vibrations that should not go as far as to be nervous-making, but here and there should indeed be unsettling. Because it's not normal that the Foreign Ministry is now where the Reichsbank was located and where gold [from Nazi victims] was stored, and later the Central Committee was located. All these levels are evidence of historical circumstances, and to constantly sense these is entirely different from sitting somewhere in a new building."[148]

At the new Finance Ministry, as well, visitors will be unable to avoid unsettling "vibrations" and echoes from the past (see figures 36–39). Housed in the former Aviation Ministry Building, it stretches an entire block along the Wilhelmstrasse—the main artery of power in imperial and Nazi Germany. With its 4.2 miles of corridors lined by 2,000 identical office cubicles, their doorways framed in sharp-edged marble and travertine, the sprawling complex exudes a spirit of hardened discipline. "Large and mighty, soldierly in its layout and in the unity of all its parts," was how an enthusiastic critic described the building of several sprawling wings and four large interior courtyards upon its completion in 1936.[149] Hermann Göring called it an impressive achievement "created in the spirit of Adolf Hitler and National Socialism."[150] The grandiosity was too much even for some fervent Nazis. Hitler's personal secretary, Martin Bormann, commented that this oversized building was no substitute for hard work and that its opulent environment suggested too much Air Force high living.[151]

Its construction within a short span of eight months was achieved by round-the-clock shifts of twelve hours each, an accomplishment that Göring hailed as a sign of the Third Reich's "joyful ability to create."[152] Like the Reichsbank design, the architecture is less historicist than the neoclassical temples devised later for Hitler by Albert Speer. Prior to Hitler's rise, Aviation Ministry architect Ernst Sagebiel had worked with Erich Mendelsohn, and the exterior of his building has a modernist rigor. The stone facade, punctuated by repeating fenestration, protruding window frames, and stark lintels, ensures a sense of solidity and tradition.

The design's military regimentation mirrors its political intent. Göring's chief aim was to rebuild the German Air Force, which had been quashed as a condition of the post–World War I Treaty of Versailles. Like Hitler at the Reich Chancellery down the street, Göring desired a building that could browbeat those who had previously humiliated Germany. "Whoever approached here felt as if he had been knocked down a peg," was how Günter Grass described the Aviation Ministry in his 1995 novel, *Ein Weites Feld* (A Broad Field). "Even state secretaries who drove by in official cars, and high-level foreign guests...had to endure an immediate sense of insignificance, if only as a feeling of spiritual suffocation."[153]

Hentrich-Petschnigg & Partners, a leading West German architectural firm, was appointed the task of renovating the Aviation Ministry Building. The firm's co-founder, Helmut Hentrich, now in retirement at age ninety-two, had a varied career, having studied under Hans Poelzig and Norman Bel Geddes before working as a member of Speer's team redesigning Berlin as the Nazi capital.[154] After the war, Hentrich designed high-rise corporate headquarters, and his firm became the German equivalent of the giant U.S. office of Skidmore, Owings & Merrill. Wolfgang Keilholz is responsible for the renovation as project director with HPP. At thirty-seven, Keilholz brings an entirely new perspective to the renovation; he spent four years working in the Atlanta-based practice of John Portman, where he designed hotels for the Hyatt chain. He claims Sagebiel's "architecture lacks every poetic, every musical element."[155] Aside from a few curving banisters on interior staircases, Sagebiel's Aviation Ministry shows no trace of the sculptural flair he might have picked up while serving as Mendelsohn's director of construction.

Like the Reichsbank, the Aviation Ministry Building has had a new tenant at each turn of Germany's difficult history since the Nazi takeover. The steel-framed building survived the bombing of Berlin with remarkably little damage, and from 1946 to 1949 the Soviet military administration located its headquarters there. In 1949, the ceremony founding the German Democratic Republic was held in the same large conference room where only a few years earlier Reichsmarschall Göring presided from a leather-padded throne. The Berlin Wall ran right up to the building's southern edge. Until the Wall's collapse in 1989, a dozen or so top East German government agencies were located in the complex, which the Communists renamed the House of Ministries. From 1991 to 1995 it was occupied by the Treuhandanstalt, the federal agency that oversaw the privatization of East German state enterprises.

All these government entities, each of a different ideological stripe, sought to modify the building in its own image. None had much success in mellowing its martial feel. The Soviet administration purged the Nazi decor, replacing it with the Soviet-style neoclassicism then in favor under Stalin. Göring's lavish reception rooms with their dark wood paneling and heavy furniture gave way to gilt and cream. The Soviets went so far as to pry out the marble floor and coffered ceilings in an effort to alter the appearance. The East Germans made their own attempt at exorcising the Aviation Ministry's ghosts by removing a massive bronze relief of Wehrmacht soldiers marching ominously eastward from the large arcade along the north facade, and substituting an equally huge painted mural depicting a joyous socialist paradise. When the building became the headquarters of the Treuhand, that agency temporarily masked the facade by draping it with large banners bearing photographic images of the anti-Communist protests that occurred outside the ministry in June 1953. The Finance Ministry will preserve the socialist mural. But in front of the arcade housing it, the ministry is considering making its own political-aesthetic statement by building a permanent memorial to workers killed in the crushing of the 1953 demonstrations. The victims were protesting against higher production quotas and demanded the resignation of the government, free elections, and the release of political prisoners.

At Keilholz's behest, the limestone facade, coated in black grime from over half a century of air pollution, has been cleaned. But landmark specialists fought hard to prevent a complete "white-washing" that would remove signs of wartime damage and eliminate shading variations of the original stonework. "One could naturally wash it so rigorously that it looks like new," said an architectural preservation consultant to the federal government, Helge Pitz. "The future tenant would have liked it to have been very clean. It will be washed but not entirely cleaned."[156] Acid rain had also eaten away at parts of the facade. Under the East Germans, damaged stone was replaced with concrete panels and crumbling lintels were propped up by makeshift wooden supports. The Finance Ministry carried out proper repairs and used new stones to replace those ravaged over the years. The window frames, daubed a drab olive under the Communists, are being repainted in a light gray-blue that will contrast with the washed stone walls. The architects hope these measures will help the building project a less severe aura.

Refurbishment of the exterior was carried out with trepidation because of unwanted mementos thought to lurk just beneath the surface. Keilholz believed that the building's Soviet-decreed "denazification" in some cases involved merely reversing carved stonework, leaving the uncarved side facing outwards, and thereby rendering invisible Nazi propaganda reliefs and insignia. He and government authorities were eager to avoid the awkward prospect of negotiations with preservationists over how and whether to conserve whatever might be unveiled in the course of restoration work. For this reason, replacement of the stone cladding proceeded gingerly, with the design team averting its gaze from what it preferred not to see revealed. "We will leave these places alone," Keilholz said of areas where reliefs were believed to lie in wait. "We are not excavators, we are pragmatists."[157]

Try as it might, the team could not prevent the past from resurfacing. In early 1997, workers in the former Aviation Ministry's basement accidentally uncovered a small brass chest interred there on October 12, 1935 to mark the completion of the building's structural frame. The chest, its cover engraved with the Luftwaffe eagle and a swastika, contained a set of architectural drawings for the ministry, crumbling proclamations in Gothic script, and curled photographs depicting Hitler, Göring, and architect Sagebiel. These items were then sent from the renovation site to the German Historical Museum to be documented and catalogued. But rather than go on display there, the box and its contents are expected to be reinterred within the walls for which they were originally intended, a time capsule from a totalitarian age deposited beneath the future machinery of a popularly elected finance minister. "This does not mean that it's being buried and hidden away, it's simply a part of the building and cannot be removed," said Christine Hoh-Slodczyk, a preservation specialist advising the government. [158]

Interior renovations also aspired to mitigate the harshness of Sagebiel's design. During the Third Reich, theatrical lighting effects in the building's entry hall served to humble those who entered the premises, as did the high placement of doorknobs at a level closer to the average shoulder than waist. Now high-tech lighting elements are being installed in the entry and corridor ceilings. The former Grosse Festsaal, which Göring had decorated with Nazi symbols, will become a ministerial conference room with sleek high-backed chairs designed by the American modernist Charles Eames. Waiting areas will be brightly lit and furnished with white Le Corbusier chairs on black rugs. The four interior courtyards, used during the Nazi era as military marching grounds, will be softened with greenery.

The addition of new artworks is also expected to go some way to adding a welcome new layer of history. Given the aesthetic predilections of the Third Reich and the communist regime, figurative works have been expressly ruled out. "The danger of misunderstanding is too great," said Keilholz. "I don't want to take the risk. We are consciously striving to avoid parallels with the 1930s. What we're doing here is confronting this building with a clear modern style. Whatever we add will be very purist, very simple, very clear. We're trying to show the building like a book of history where you can read the pages that show what happened already, and we just add a few pages and write our own story. We're trying not to erase anything that's happened. It's almost like an injection of a new philosophy to the building. We are trying to start this transformation. The user will have to finish it."[159]

Keilholz thus rejects the notion that the buildings should be barred from reuse by the Federal Republic. "The guilt is born by people," he said. "But today one must respect that guilt emanated from this building. The user who will now occupy this building must know that. And by occupying such a building one takes on an obligation, one that is greater than if one were just to tear down the building."[160] For Germany to destroy the Nazi structures would be tantamount to suppressing the past, and it is far preferable for the government to try and live with them as best as possible. History cannot be changed by negating it architecturally. "The important thing," Building Minister Töpfer observed, "is the spirit that reigns in a building today and in the future."[161]

Berlin's architecture itself is not to blame for the terrible crimes once organized from the German capital. The stones themselves are not guilty. Punishing these buildings for what happened there would be like tearing down Canterbury Cathedral for the murder of Thomas à Becket. On the other hand, political architecture cannot be entirely separated from the context in which it arose. It is instilled with meaning related to its past, happy or not. The integration of the burdensome legacy into the framework of a democratic capital and the manner in which its history will be conveyed to future generations pose important tests of German political character. For this reason, the refurbishment and reuse of these buildings must entail more than aesthetic attempts to neutralize the designs that the Nazis regarded as an effective means towards achieving their dictatorial goals.

COMMUNIST RELICS

If German politicians worried that reusing Nazi-era buildings in the capital might complicate their country's reputation abroad, domestically they were even more at pains to distance themselves from the built legacy of the German Democratic Republic. Communism was a more vivid and direct memory for the electorate than the Third Reich. So despite the evolution towards "recycling" Nazi-era buildings as modern-day ministries, there was strong resistance to applying this practice to the most prominent state architectural projects of the only recently defunct East German regime. In cases where East German buildings were accepted for official reuse, the renovations often involved total transformations of their appearance. For instance, when the Bundestag turned the former Ministry for Foreign Trade and the Ministry for People's Education into offices for its own members, both were stripped to their structural frames and rebuilt from the outside in.

In contrast to the perdurable former Reichsbank and Aviation Ministry Building, the Communist-era buildings had the reputation of being decidedly dingy and poorly crafted. This was reinforced by harsh assessments of East German architecture delivered by Western critics. "The profession of architecture had ceased to exist in the GDR," wrote Manfred Sack in summing up its design achievements since 1949. "With a few isolated exceptions ... the next forty years saw no architecture in East Germany worthy of the designation."[162] Given the high degree of standardized construction and material shortages under the Communist centralized economy, there was truth to this judgment. The sweeping condemnation typified dismissive West German attitudes towards the legacy of their fellow Germans.

A notable exemption was made in the case of East German buildings from the neoclassic period of the early 1950s. This was largely a question of style and shifts in architectural taste, since the Stalinist regime that created them was even more rigid and orthodox than the one that constructed the more modernist Marx-Engels-Platz. But by the 1990s, the grandiose apartments along the Stalinallee, now the Karl-Marx-Allee, were hailed as great urban architecture by fashionable foreign architects like Philip Johnson and Aldo Rossi. Johnson called the former Stalinallee "real city planning in the grand manner."[163] Rather than being regarded as the remnants of an unjust political system, the buildings were viewed by some as admirable aesthetic progenitors of postmodernism. The Karl-Marx-Allee apartment houses were privatized in 1993, and much of the boulevard underwent investor-funded restoration.

Elsewhere in Berlin, there were fears that the modernist architecture and urban planning of the fallen Communist regime would blemish the shining new countenance of the unified capital. "What difference does the postmodern splendor of the Parliament Buildings, the Foreign Ministry, or the Chancellery make when in front and behind them stretch amorphous and shabby urban spaces?" queried the influential weekly *Die Zeit*.[164] The government acknowledged the sheer impossibility of tearing down all of the buildings put up by the East German government. But it proposed fundamentally altering the urban environment by increasing Berlin's density and filling in the vast empty windswept spaces that were commonplace in the old Communist capital.

The ensemble of East German state buildings around the Marx-Engels-Platz bore the brunt of the official disapprobation. In 1993, the federal government sponsored an architectural competition to redesign the square and the surrounding area, known as the Spreeinsel (island in the Spree) since it is bounded by that river and its smaller tributaries. The competition guidelines formally left the fate of the Communist-era buildings up to the entrants, while hinting at the government's true aspirations by urging a restoration of the historic street pattern. For this reason, critics accused Bonn of exploiting the professional legitimacy conferred by a design competition as a means to bolster top-level plans to eradicate East German architectural remains.

The contest drew a dizzying 1,106 submissions. Brazilians, Japanese, Australians, and Saudi Arabians were among the architects of fifty-eight nations vying against German colleagues to redesign what was Berlin's most ancient core. First prize was awarded to a thirty-five-year-old West Berlin architect, Bernd Niebuhr, who did propose demolishing the Council of State Building, along with the Palace of the Republic and the East German Foreign Ministry Building. In his scheme, the vacated Marx-Engels-Platz would then be covered by a vast quadrangular conference center, library, and exhibition hall. This complex had the size and shape of the vanished Royal Palace; it occupied the palace's footprint and centered around an oval courtyard.

The competition results stirred outrage among a broad cross-section of architects and urban planners who saw the democratic government behaving little differently than the Communists had when they ordered the palace's demolition. "We find it unacceptable that buildings that have become a part of urban history are being erased from memory precisely because they are historically burdened," said Cornelius Hertling, president of the Berlin Chamber of Architects, an umbrella organization of architects from both parts of the unified city. "History and identity are thereby being eradicated."[165]

In June 1994, over one hundred respected architects, historians, and landmark preservationists signed a petition protesting the elimination of the Council of State Building. More than half of the signatories were from former West Germany. This was a calculated move. "We were of the opinion that it had to be a majority of Westerners in order for it to be politically successful," said petition co-organizer and urban historian Harald Bodenschatz. "We are still in the remarkable situation whereby projects that are advocated primarily by Eastern colleagues are much more likely to be denigrated and brushed aside."[166] The architectural consultant's report prepared for the Berlin city government had already found the Council of State Building to be eminently worthy of preservation. "It represents not just any state building, but the most important state building of the former GDR," the report said.[167]

The timing of the protests coincided with official worries that the electorate might balk at the increasingly high financial cost of unification. These anxieties prompted the government to reign in its original plans to build entirely new ministries in Berlin, and eventually led to a partial change of heart regarding the government's plans to dismantle the East German buildings. In effect, the results of the Spreeinsel competition were nullified shortly after being made public. The Council of State Building then got a stay of execution when Building Minister Töpfer moved his own Berlin headquarters into its upper floors. The ground floor conference and reception rooms were converted into the federal government's information center for capital planning. The generously proportioned spaces, designed for formal state occasions hosted by Communist leaders, proved equally well suited for architectural exhibitions and symposia.

What once had been a guarded preserve of top-level Communist chiefs became a highly accessible public building and a popular meeting place for open debate about Berlin's future. Culminating the remarkable symbolic transformation of the once-threatened building, Chancellor Kohl announced in February 1997 that he would temporarily move his offices there from Bonn in May 1999, while he or his successor awaits completion of the new Schultes-designed Chancellery, scheduled to open January 1, 2000. Kohl decided to take up the provisional quarters in order to ensure that the government stuck to its timetable for completing the capital's transfer before the end of the millennium. In a telling sign of lingering ambivalence about contact with the physical remnants of the Communist state, the chancellor and his aides avoided referring to the Council of State Building by that name. Nor did they refer to it as Marx-Engels-Platz 1, its postal address for decades, but as 1 Palace Square

(Schlossplatz 1), its latest incarnation. Kohl also termed it "a place where never in my wildest dreams could I have foreseen that I would one day work."[168]

Though Bonn's reversal of plans to raze the Council of State Building represented a major victory for preservationists, it still did not lead to widespread acceptance for the adjacent structures. Removing them from sight continued to preoccupy many politicians in both Bonn and Berlin. In 1995, the white aluminum-clad Foreign Ministry became the first building erected by the German Democratic Republic to fall prey to the wrecker's ball since unification *(see figure 41)*. Its overblown dimensions, in clear violation of the city's traditional height limits, made it an easy target for demolition. Mindful that Communists had been accused of sweeping history out of view with similar actions, the government took care to use a bizarre linguistic contortion, *"Rückbau"* (a newspeak term meaning "reverse building") rather than *"Abriß"* (demolition) to refer to the Foreign Ministry's removal. The task was completed with scant protest or regret. The Berlin newspaper *BZ*, a popular tabloid whose readership included former East Germans, bade farewell to the bulky Communist Foreign Ministry with the headline: "Bye, Bye Clunker. No One Sheds Any Tears Over You."[169]

Just as it ensured the preservation of the former Stalinallee, 1990s architectural taste helped ease the way for the ministry's removal. A private citizens' group called for replacing it with a resurrection of Schinkel's Bauakademie, the Prussian state architectural school that had stood on the site from 1835 until 1961. Regarded as Schinkel's first "modern" building designed according to functionalist dictates, the four-story Bauakademie was a cube of flaming red bricks. Its window areas and door frames were surrounded by ornamented terra-cotta panels that were richly illustrated with carved reliefs. Some portrayed the concept of architecture as both an art and a science; others depicted the qualities demanded of its practitioners. Because the once trend-setting Bauakademie enjoyed cult status among architects and urban planners, many of the same people who indignantly protested against razing other East German landmarks readily turned a blind eye to the elimination of the Foreign Ministry. But in the absence of funds to pay for rebuilding the Bauakademie, the vacated ministry site was covered for the time being with grass and a statue of Schinkel.

Far more disputed was the government's decision to eliminate the Palace of the Republic that covered part of the site along Marx-Engels-Platz where the Hohenzollern Royal Palace stood until 1950. The government ordered the building shut in 1990 after finding it contaminated by large amounts of asbestos fireproofing. But East Germans saw this justification for the closure as a mere political pretext, since another equally ugly convention and entertainment center that also dated from the 1970s, the Internationale Congress Centrum in West Berlin, continued to operate despite its own asbestos contamination. Outside the shuttered Palace of the Republic, placard-carrying protesters demanded that it be reopened. In the meantime, the terraces surrounding the building became a skateboarders' paradise. With no more party apparatchiks left to park their cars in the Marx-Engels-Platz, the disused square was temporarily taken up by an itinerant amusement park with carnival rides and refreshment stands.

No sooner was the Palace of the Republic sealed to the public than a campaign by West Germans to replace it with a replica of the original royal residence began. Enthusiasm for this ambitious undertaking was spurred on by a spate of books that appeared in the wake of unification containing photographs and drawings of old Berlin. These burnished the image of the pre-World War I monarchical age as the time of the city's greatest beauty and splendor. Nostalgia for that bygone day often reflected aesthetic and political naiveté. "Everyone, whether left or right, wants a beautiful city, apart from a few intellectuals who say we must continue to suffer from our Nazi-era sins and that these must remain visible," said Annette Ahme, the head of the Society for Historical Berlin, a leading backer of the campaign to rebuild the palace. "We see that as totally perverse. It is very important for the history of National Socialism to be taught and remembered in museums, concentration camps, memorials, and so on. But it makes no sense to overload the city with these pedagogical things and have every building and empty lot proclaim forever, 'You evil Germans. You made the war and now you must put up with an ugly city.' The city must be beautiful so that people will be happy and they will not repeat these mistakes."[170]

The view that Berlin was more pleasing in its prewar manifestation got a major boost when in 1993 a life-size canvas mockup of the royal residence was raised upon scaffolding that covered much of the glass-faced Communist structure. The trompe l'oeil canvas panels, painted by the French artist Catherine Feff and a crew of Parisian art students, extended into the Marx-Engels-Platz and roughly reproduced the exterior of the Prussian royal residence designed in the eighteenth century by Andreas Schlüter and Johann Friedrich Eosander von Göthe *(see figure 43).*

Feff had constructed similar public installations elsewhere. In Paris she covered the Place de la Concorde's obelisk with an enormous trompe l'oeil radio to commemorate the fiftieth anniversary of Charles de Gaulle's broadcast calling for resistance to the Nazi occupation. But what exactly was the message broadcast by the fake palace in Berlin? Did it imply that Germans had overthrown a Communist dictatorship in order to restore the monarchy or the hierarchical society that existed during its heyday? Or did it suggest that one could undo the misdeeds of East German leader Walter Ulbricht by repeating his act of architectural destruction on the same site over forty years later?

The mural's bright yellow panels enlivened the area around the Palace of the Republic for nearly a year. By the time they were removed, the specter of the Royal Palace had left a lasting impression on Berliners. One hundred and eighty thousand people visited an exhibition held within the canvas facade that documented the vanished building and proposals to rebuild it. The project's sponsor, Hamburg businessman Wilhelm von Boddien, estimated that it would cost $600 million to tear down the Communist-era building and reconstruct the shell of the

Royal Palace in its place. Rebuilding the lavish interiors, including the throne room and ornate ballrooms, would have pushed this figure much higher. As a consequence, this option was never seriously considered by the German government.

The last monarch to have used the palace, Kaiser Wilhelm II, left Berlin for exile in Holland in 1918. Little had been heard from the Hohenzollern dynasty until 1991, when the family oversaw the reburial of Frederick the Great at a royal residence in Potsdam, which came under Red Army control in 1945. His remains had been transferred to West Germany by the family after World War II, and they opted to return them when the Communists had been removed from power. Chancellor Kohl's decision to attend the reburial in effect rendered it a state occasion and stirred disquiet among liberal Germans, many of whom were equally troubled by the symbolic ramifications of the palace mockup. It was not so much fear of a royal restoration—that topic was never even broached—as German anxiety about pride in the past and suspicion of the cultivation of tradition. Deeply distrustful of themselves, many Germans panicked that even a fleeting revival of national spirit could be a slippery slope. Kohl took a different view, saying that Germany "needs to stand before our entire history," rather than demonize its past, a statement indicating impatience with those the chancellor saw as focusing too much attention on the twelve years of Nazi rule.[171]

The surviving members of the Hohenzollern family were largely absent from the palace debate, although a collateral descendant, Ferdinand von Hohenzollern, now a Berlin architect in his late thirties, was among those competing to redesign the Spreeinsel. His proposal avoided calling for reconstructing the palace once occupied by his ancestors; instead, von Hohenzollern figured among those advocating a modern convention center on the site. According to his design, which placed in the top fifty entries but won no actual prize, the convention center would be built after razing the Palace of the Republic and the East German Foreign Ministry Building.[172]

For Berliners, the fleeting experience of the original palace's massing via the mockup underscored the importance of the site and its role in determining the city's identity and historical self-understanding. The Royal Palace had been a crucial landmark marking the eastern terminus of Unter den Linden. Whatever structure occupied that locale—be it the copper-colored reflective panels of the Communist's palace or the eighteenth-century ornamentation of the Hohenzollern residence—would be visible from the Brandenburg Gate in the west and Alexanderplatz in the east.

What also became more clear through the mockup was the degree to which the original palace's form determined the layout of the surrounding area, which had served as the symbolic center of German power for centuries. This included the position of the Berlin Cathedral, the Lustgarten, and the Altes Museum. With the palace gone, this spatial arrangement lost its coherence. "Ulbricht not only took the palace from us," said Barbara Jakubeit, who became Berlin municipal building director in 1996. "He destroyed the entire urban space. It's an urbanistic problem. One can't get rid of the Palace of the Republic for ideological reasons. It's not that it's so ugly that we have to tear it down. We would drown in rubble if we were to tear down everything in the Federal Republic that is not beautiful. But in such an important place, one must be concerned about the urbanistic concept. And this building is simply totally wrong for the site."[173]

Proponents of rebuilding the palace cited Poland's 1970s reconstruction of its royal palace in Warsaw, as well as the reconstruction in the 1950s of another Hohenzollern residence, the Charlottenburg Palace in West Berlin. Many other buildings along Unter den Linden that had their genesis under the monarchy were also rebuilt by the Communists after suffering wartime damage. Defending her desire to reconstruct the palace against criticism that it would lack historical authenticity, Jakubeit said, "In music, if one has the score then one can perform concerts and play the music over and over again. If I have the text of a book I can republish it. And if I have a Maillol original, and he has authorized it, then I can cast a copy. . . . What makes the art of architecture so precious that if its score still exists it can't be reproduced?"[174]

In addition to those advocating the reconstruction of the Royal Palace and those who wanted to preserve the Palace of the Republic, there were others who regarded the Communist-era building as simply an inadequate work of architecture for such a pivotal place in the city. They advocated a modern structure. But there was some doubt that contemporary architecture would be able to rise to the challenge. "The superiority of the canvas Berlin palace over the actual modern structures surrounding it was a shock to realize," wrote the urban planner Dieter Hoffmann-Axthelm. "But it was not the superiority of a staged illusion or of historical decor; it was the superiority of a historical appearance that can no longer be restored—a historical fate, in a word, that we would do good to accept. The design process goes on, but no one should continue to pat himself on the back and imagine he could do it as well as [Andreas] Schlüter."[175]

As historian Brian Ladd observed in his book *The Ghosts of Berlin*, rival nostalgias were at work here.[176] While West Germans looked back to the beauty of a misty monarchical age, former East Germans fondly recalled their leisure hours spent at the Palace of the Republic and in doing so mused that the life under Communism had not been all that bad. For these East Germans, the threatened removal of one of their former capital's prime landmarks came amid a disorienting series of street name changes and the elimination of other historic plaques and markers set down by the vanished Communist government. Advocates of retaining the building cited the apolitical nature of the "people's palace" open to all. But it was never so clear-cut. Certainly, a range of entertainment—including performances by acrobatic teams, rock musicians and jazz bands, art exhibitions, and festivals highlighting regional culinary specialties—had been offered then. But the program for January 1984 shows that much of this fare had a heavy ideological tint. Its listing for a three-day

"Rock for Peace" music extravaganza assailed Alexander Haig, former commander of NATO forces in Europe, for his "attack on human existence through the confrontational policies of the most aggressive circles of the USA and their NATO puppets."[177]

The Palace of the Republic's politicized reputation fed West German antipathy to its preservation. Chancellor Kohl himself advocated its demolition to make way for a reconstruction of the Royal Palace facade, as did the Berlin division of his Christian Democratic Union. Many West German advocates of the palace reconstruction were determined to seal their victory over the exhausted Communist system, as if they were uncertain that their cold-war triumph would be secure until they had eradicated the architectural reminders. Destroying the East German remains was seen as a step towards expunging the evil of communism itself. "In the worldwide political conflict that lies behind us, what was ultimately at stake was thwarting the advance of this domination," the historian Joachim Fest wrote of communist ideology. "If the destruction of the palace was supposed to be the symbol of its victory, then reconstruction would be the symbol of its failure."[178]

A joint committee representing the federal government and the city of Berlin did decide to order the removal of the asbestos, a step required for either refurbishing or destroying the Palace of the Republic. The committee also invited private investors to submit proposals for commercial use of the square, and the question of what to do with the extinct socialist forum was further debated in the Bundestag, in countless newspaper articles, and in public symposia. After the palace mockup was removed, the newspaper *Berliner Tagesspiegel* ran a twelve-week series of proposals by a dozen leading architects for redesigning the square. Many of these urged a compromise between old and new by incorporating the Palace of the Republic into part of a reconstructed palace facade. President Roman Herzog, advocating a middle ground, supported this position. "It should not be a question of the palace versus the Palace of the Republic," the German head of state said, "but a bit of the palace and a bit of the Palace of the Republic, and above all something brand new."[179] This approach sounded less like a reasoned middle ground than a feeble solution for an irresolute nation.

The symbolic emptiness of the competing visions for the square came into even sharper relief as unified Berlin shifted its locus of power and its primary architectural embodiment westwards from the Spreeinsel to the Spreebogen. It will be on this spot, bounded by the bend in the Spree River, rather than on the historic terrain where kings, kaisers, and communists reigned for centuries, that the new political apex will arise with the Reichstag and the Federal Strip. The Spreeinsel remains urbanistically important but, at least for now, devoid of real content. Suggestions that the area be put to use as home to a new convention center, hotel, art gallery, or library ring hollow and unconvincing since these functions are amply fulfilled elsewhere in the city.

Like the Nazi buildings, the East German structures are repositories for the long-term memory of the political and social conditions that created them. The preservation of at least some key examples of communist-era architecture could help promote an understanding of a common past among Germans. After all, both the Federal Republic and the German Democratic Republic arose from the ashes of the Third Reich. Hard as it is for some Germans to accept, the Palace of the Republic represents a heritage they now share.

NORMAN FOSTER'S REICHSTAG
ILLUMINATING SHADOWS OF THE PAST

No structure in Germany has a more potent or more turbulent presence than the Reichstag *(see figure 44)*. Shortly after the Bundestag's 1991 decision to move back to Berlin, the parliamentary body quietly and with little controversy voted to use the notorious building as its new home. The consensus surrounding the plan proved short-lived. At a 1992 Bundestag-sponsored colloquium to discuss overhauling the Reichstag, it was depicted as a bombastic, war-scarred fossil, the scene of Germany's darkest hours, an unwelcome symbol of democracy's failure to grow deep roots under either the monarchy or the succeeding Weimar republic. The argument continues to this day.

Critics repeatedly disparaged the Reichstag with the word "Wilhelmine," by which they meant that it epitomized the saber-rattling bluster of the last German emperor, Kaiser Wilhelm II. Architect Günter Behnisch, frustrated that his message-laden Bonn parliament was being abandoned so soon after its completion, compared the Bundestag's decision to reconvene in the century-old Reichstag to the federal president taking the Kaiser's uniform out of mothballs and wearing it in the 1990s.[180] Pressure from conservative parliamentarians to restore the Reichstag cupola only inflamed censure of the building, for critics saw this crowning element as a blown-up version of the spiked military helmet worn by the Kaiser's troops in World War I.

The actual history of the much-maligned building at times has been misconstrued. When the Red Army conquered Berlin at the end of World War II, its soldiers signaled that the German enemy had been defeated by unfurling the Soviet flag not atop the Reich Chancellery, from which Hitler controlled much of Europe, but over the battered Reichstag *(see figure 45)*. For the Soviets, and many others who fought against Nazism, the

Reichstag had come to embody fascist terror ever since Hitler used a 1933 fire that engulfed the building as a pretext to impose emergency rule. In the 1990s, advocates of reusing the building as home to the Bundestag tried to set the record straight, pointing out that Nazi crimes and atrocities were planned not in the parliament but inside other Berlin structures. Hitler only once set foot inside it as Germany's chancellor, and the fateful vote by which the Reichstag committed constitutional suicide, approving the so-called Enabling Act that handed its authority over to the Führer, took place not in the Reichstag itself but in the nearby Kroll Opera where the legislature reconvened after the suspicious blaze.

The building, its premises no longer in demand as a parliament, languished for most of the Third Reich's duration, though it was periodically put to use in the late 1930s to stage Nazi propaganda exhibitions like "Bolshevism Unmasked" and "The Wandering Jew." It slumbered in near ruins for many years after World War II, suffering another blow when its tottering cupola was torn down as a safety hazard in 1954 *(see figure 46)*. Most of its elaborate exterior decorative elements and sculpture were either blown to pieces by the war or were removed soon afterwards. A simple interior renovation, leaving off the cupola, was carried out by the modernist architect Paul Baumgarten in the 1960s. Baumgarten made no attempt to recreate the Reichstag's original interior, but instead implanted a spare, white, modernist chamber into the nineteenth-century shell. This space, along with the unassuming new foyers, reception areas, and hallways, was designed in the same spirit as the early Schwippert-Witte parliament in Bonn.

The Bundestag financed the 1960s refurbishment with the aim of holding some sessions in Berlin as a proof of its intent to eventually return there. But after the Soviet Union angrily protested that this presaged West German revanchism, the Bundestag shied away from holding full-fledged meetings in the renovated building. The cold war thus kept it sidelined as nothing more than a tourist attraction and home to a government-sponsored historical exhibition. Unification changed all that. "The arsonists of

February 27, 1933 should not have the last word," argued Oscar Schneider, a former building minister and an architectural advisor to Chancellor Kohl, who pushed for a faithful restoration of the cupola and charged its opponents with distorting a symbol of democratic sovereignty into an architectural mark of Cain. "A policy that shuns historical orientation and responsibility destroys the self-identity of the nation."[181]

The Reichstag—the name translates as Imperial Diet—provoked equally vehement condemnation when it was first built. After the founding of the unified empire in 1871, it took nearly a quarter of a century for the legislature to acquire a permanent home. When it finally did, the Reichstag ended up on a less-than-central site well away from the Royal Palace and outside the medieval wall of the city, just northwest of the Brandenburg Gate. Wilhelm I laid the foundation stone in 1884, and his grandson and successor Wilhelm II dedicated the finished edifice in 1894. Even then, formal openings of the parliamentary session took place at the palace rather than in the Reichstag itself. The venue mirrored the true balance of power in a young nation-state where popular sovereignty never gained a foothold. Although all German males twenty-five years of age and over were entitled to elect Reichstag members by secret ballot, the legislature's prerogatives were greatly restricted. The monarch retained the sole right to appoint the chancellor and keep him in office, leaving the Reichstag to reinforce more the appearance of democracy than its reality.

The Reichstag's architect, Paul Wallot, bemoaned his difficulty in designing a national building amid a lack of consensus on what constituted a national German architectural style. For decades prior to the empire's foundation, German architects and theorists fiercely debated the appropriate style for public buildings. Many looked to the past for security and tradition. The art historian and archaeologist Johann Joachim Winckelmann appealed in his writings for the creation of a Germanic artistic culture embracing that of ancient Greece, while the architect and theorist Heinrich Hübsch argued that the marble temples of Greek antiquity were inappropriate to Germany's climate, building materials, and traditions. Wallot's messy Reichstag synthesis of baroque and Italian Renaissance elements was a product of this ongoing confusion.

In the absence of a national style, Wallot used ornate decorations to proclaim the building's importance. To a large extent, these embellishments glorify not parliamentary democracy but the successful military campaigns of Prussia's Hohenzollern dynasty and its role in unifying the Reich. A twenty-foot-tall sculpture of the female embodiment of the Teutonic nation, entitled "Germania in the Saddle," loomed high atop the heavy facade of Silesian sandstone, along with sixteen other allegorical figures posted on the four castlelike corner towers. Above the main entry was a curious blend of imagery from the medieval Holy Roman Empire and that of the later German amalgamation: a relief of the dragon-slaying St. George bore the face of the Reich's founding chancellor, Otto von Bismarck. Inside, frescoes of the imperial eagle and coats of arms adorned the ceilings above floors of inlaid marble.

Wallot's cupola of glass and steel presented a more modern and progressive image. Advocates of the Reichstag's reuse as home to the Bundestag argued that it was intended to be as much a political assertion as a decorative element. Rising slightly higher than the dome of the Royal Palace, the Reichstag cupola joined the domes of the Berlin Cathedral as the dominant elements on the turn-of-the-century capital skyline. Recent supporters of rebuilding the cupola said that with it the legislature had architecturally expressed a bid for parliamentary sovereignty, a force to be reckoned with along with church and crown. Wilhelm II, hardly an exponent of legislative democracy, termed the cupola "the height of tastelessness." He sneered at the building and the institution it housed as the "imperial monkey house."[182]

In 1993, the Berlin architectural historian Tilmann Buddensieg made a convincing case that the Reichstag dome was an explicitly democratic construction. He argued that Wallot intentionally made his cupola different in material and form from the rounded domes of the past, using a square vaulted shape with a clearly visible steel framework. When the cupola was unveiled, the architects Hermann Muthesius and Bruno Taut hailed it as a form of design liberation. The Reichstag cupola went on to become a model for fin-de-siècle civic architecture throughout Europe, including new train stations and exhibition halls in Dresden, Nuremberg, Lucerne, Antwerp, and Bucharest.[183]

But the Reichstag's aspirations for democratic sovereignty were clearly frustrated. Nearly two decades after the building's completion passed before the words "*Dem Deutschen Volke*" (To the German People) were affixed to its pediment. The delay stemmed from opposition to the declaration by Wilhelm II, who preferred that it read "To German Unity." More cynical observers of Reichstag proceedings proposed variants like "Entry Barred to the German People" or "Beware of Pickpockets."[184] The raising of the populist dedication in bronze letters each two feet high came just before Christmas Day 1916, foreshadowing the fall of the monarchy by a little less than two years. From a Reichstag window on November 9, 1918, the Social Democratic parliamentarian Philip Scheidemann proclaimed the death of the old order and the birth of a German republic. The succeeding entity was known as the Weimar Republic since legislators convened to write its constitution not in Berlin, where violent protests engulfed the Reichstag, but at a safe remove in Weimar, where they stayed until coming back to the capital in 1920.

The ultimate failure of parliamentarism in interwar Germany lends a poignancy to the building, which can perhaps best be viewed as embodying the country's thwarted democratic hopes and the belated remorse felt by many of those who acquiesced in their suppression. Thus the wrapping of the Reichstag by the Bulgarian-born artist Christo in July 1994 was applauded not only as an extraordinary aesthetic spectacle but as a way of reconsecrating this history-soiled hulk for a better future. Chancellor Kohl and other conservatives had unsuccessfully sought to block Christo and his wife, Jeanne-Claude, from encasing the building in a million square feet of silvery fabric, arguing that the Reichstag was too important a national monument with which to trifle. The Bundestag voted 292 to 223 to allow the endeavor after an emotional debate in which parliamentarian Peter Conradi countered that the artist would turn the German parliament into a "precious gift" made even more valuable by its wrapping. "With this act," Conradi said, "we want to send a positive sign, a beautiful, illuminating signal, that fosters courage and hope and exudes self-confidence."[185] As soon as Christo's shimmering bands of polypropylene material were removed, construction began on a design by Sir Norman Foster of Britain to redo the building as the new home for the 672-member Bundestag.

Foster, the architect of modernist skyscrapers for Hong Kong and Frankfurt banks as well as renovations of historic structures like London's Royal Academy and the British Museum, gutted Wallot's Reichstag to retrofit the place in his high-tech machine aesthetic. Translucent roofing, glass elevators, and enlarged windows will flood as much light as possible into the heavy stone building as part of his effort to make "democracy visible." The prescription was a radical one, and in many eyes it showed that Bonn politicians were bent on transforming Wallot's relic into a contemporary transparent glass house by any means possible. In the view of one leading German architecture critic, the Bundestag members treated the Reichstag as an invalid, entrusting it to the "intensive care unit of high-tech architecture where, under a thousand needles and wires, it is undergoing even more mutation into that undying monstrosity of whom one allegedly has such a great fear."[186] Indeed, the building had housed a functioning, if never fully healthy, parliamentary democracy for only about a dozen years after 1918 and, in the wake of Christo's ephemeral vision, Foster was called upon to undertake permanent surgical interventions to bring new symbolic meaning to the structure.

The choice of Foster was in itself a symbolic gesture, for it would be hard to imagine France, Britain, or the United States hiring a foreign citizen to design a new national legislature. Germany invited fourteen leading foreign architects to compete in the Reichstag competition. They included Foster, Austria's Hans Hollein, Japan's Fumihiko Maki, Spain's

José Rafael Moneo, and Italy's Aldo Rossi judged against seventy-five German firms. By enlisting the aid of a star architect from abroad, the Bundestag sidestepped charges of nationalist triumphalism in the refurbishment of the country's most prominent piece of political architecture. "There was perhaps some anxiety that if we did it in a purely German manner we would have taken a whack," said Dietmar Kansy, chairman of the Bundestag's Building Committee.[187]

Given the intense anxiety over the building's image and reputation, the jury seemed uncertain about which design would best respond to the Bundestag's needs while at the same time turn the Reichstag into a new and convincing emblem of parliamentary democracy. As in the case of the new Chancellery, the jury was unable to select a clear winner. Instead, it awarded three first prizes in February 1993; to Foster, the Dutch architect Pi de Bruijn, and the Spaniard Santiago Calatrava. All three foreigners were in tune with German ambivalence about the original structure. De Bruijn, who had designed a new addition to the Dutch national parliament in the Hague, preserved Wallot's building but housed the legislature's plenary chamber completely outside of the Reichstag itself in a new bowl-like structure placed on an adjacent terrace. Calatrava redefined the Reichstag's silhouette by crowning the shell of Wallot's building with a delicate glass dome capable of opening up like a flower. For his part, Foster gutted the interior while preserving the exterior in a manner that he said rendered it "present but void."[188]

Foster's initial design called for erecting an enormous translucent canopy supported by twenty slender pillars high over the building *(see figure 47)*. This dramatic solution, he said, corresponded to "the need for a new symbol, a symbol that corresponds to our age, a new image of an open future." Foster had closely studied Behnisch's plan in Bonn and was aware of the German reluctance to exalt political power there. With this in mind, Foster proposed a public piazza or forum around the perimeter of the Reichstag at the same elevation as the plenary chamber. "It respects the needs and function of government but places government on the same level and under the same roof as the people it serves," he said.[189] The plan seemed to imply that the notion of democracy embodied in Wallot's building was inadequate to provide an open democratic forum for a unified Germany at the end of the twentieth century.

After all the enthusiasm it elicited among jurors in the first round of the competition, some Bundestag members grumbled that Foster's enormous canopy gave the Reichstag the look of an oversized gas station or airplane hanger.[190] Foster, de Bruijn, and Calatrava were then asked to submit reworked designs for a second stage of the competition in which the space requirements were substantially altered. Foster won with a far more modest proposal that discarded both piazza and canopy to leave the parliament raised up on its original pedestal and newly encased underneath a flat roof of clear glass within the existing Reichstag walls. "We do not recommend raising this roof artificially above the skyline of the present building," he said of the revised submission, "either as a new dome or a version of our original umbrella. To do so poses no technical problems beyond that of yet further cost. . . . However, at a philosophical level we question the need, for purely symbolic purposes, of going higher than necessary and spending more money for questionable effect."[191]

Foster ended up having to do exactly that. Like Wallot a century earlier, Foster experienced how difficult it was to work with a legislative body as his patron, which meant having several hundred deputies and ministers peering over his shoulder as he drafted. The Foster design that the Bundestag eventually approved and built was the result of countless compromises with what was in effect a multiheaded client. It was not so much the clear conception of one architect, backed up by a team of several dozen others, as the partly muddled outcome of conflicting crosscurrents of the democratic political process.

Within the Bundestag, architectural ambitions and tastes broke along party lines. Intraparliamentary bickering ensued. Conservative members were prepared to accept the logical simplicity of Foster's architecture for the Reichstag interior. But outside the building, they fought avidly for a

31 Reichsbank President Hjalmar Schacht (at right with hammer in hand), accompanied by Adolf
Hitler at the cornerstone-laying ceremony for the new Reichsbank, May 5, 1934. "Our opponents
will come to realize it, but above all our followers must know it: our buildings are built with the
aim of strengthening...authority," Hitler declared.

32 The cornerstone-laying ceremony for the Reichsbank on May 5, 1934. A model of the building is
at the bottom left and Adolf Hitler stands before a microphone as the crowd salutes.

33 Former Reichsbank, later used as headquarters of the East German Communist Party, will become
the Foreign Ministry of unified Germany. Its subterranean vault, used to stockpile goods stolen
from concentration camp victims, will become the ministry archive.

34 Drawing showing court between the Foreign Ministry addition (left) and the former Reichsbank (right) where Foreign Ministers of democratic Germany will receive visiting dignitaries in the shadow of Nazi architecture.

35 Atrium of the Foreign Ministry addition—designed by Thomas Müller and Ivan Reimann—to the former Reichsbank Building with a view towards a neo-Gothic church by Karl Friedrich Schinkel. The drawing evokes a famed 1829 sketch by Schinkel for the Altes Museum in Berlin.

36 Hermann Göring's Aviation Ministry, designed by Ernst Sagebiel. "Large and mighty, soldierly in its layout and in the unity of its parts," wrote a pro-Nazi critic when the building was completed in 1936.

37 Aviation Ministry as envisioned by Hentrich-Petschnigg & Partners after renovation as the Finance Ministry of unified Germany. The renovation will involve cleaning and repairing the facade and landscaping—moves that are aimed at helping the Nazi-era building project a less-severe presence.

38 Grosse Festsaal of Göring's Aviation Ministry in 1938. The huge eagle and swastika, along with the stone flooring and coffered ceiling, were removed by the Soviets after World War II in an attempt to "de-Nazify" the architecture.

39 The former Grosse Festsaal of Aviation Ministry as envisioned by Hentrich-Petschnigg & Partners when converted into the ministerial conference room in unified Germany's Finance Ministry. Chairs by the American modernist Charles Eames fill the former ballroom.

40 Model of East German Foreign Ministry. Designed by Josef Kaiser and completed in 1967, the building was created to be big enough to serve as Foreign Ministry of both Germanys under a Soviet-favored unification plan.

41 The East German Foreign Ministry was the first Communist-era building to be felled by a wrecker's ball after unification. The task was completed with scant protest or regret in 1995. "Bye, Bye Clunker. No One Sheds Any Tears Over You," read one Berlin newspaper headline.

42 East Germany's Palace of the Republic, designed by Heinz Graffunder and completed in 1976 on the site of Berlin's former Royal Palace. Unified Germany shut the building in 1990 and considered tearing it down to rebuild a replica of the palace that the Communists destroyed in 1950.

43 A canvas mock-up of the Royal Palace hung against the facade of the Palace of the Republic in 1993 as part of a campaign to rebuild the imperial residence. The trompe l'oeil palace stood for nearly a year and evoked nostalgia for the prewar capital.

44 Reichstag designed by Paul Wallot and completed in 1894. Kaiser Wilhelm II denounced its glass and steel cupola as "the height of tastelessness" and the parliament it contained as the "imperial monkey house."

45 Soviet soldier hoisting red flag over battered Reichstag in 1945. For the Soviets and many others, the Reichstag had come to embody fascist terror.

46 Reichstag in 1990. The building was severely damaged during World War II and its tottering cupola was removed as a safety hazard in 1954.

47 Sir Norman Foster's original design for the Reichstag renovation called for erecting an enormous translucent canopy, supported by twenty slender pillars, over the building.

48 After conservative German politicians pressed Sir Norman Foster to restore the Reichstag dome, the architect experimented with dozens of alternatives, projecting them on the building like wigs on a mannequin.

49 Computer rendering showing the dome of the renovated Reichstag. Designed by Sir Norman Foster, it contains spiral viewing ramps open to the public, thereby placing German citizens symbolically above the politicians answerable to them.

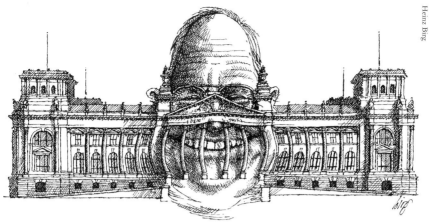

Heinz Birg

50 Caricature of Chancellor Helmut Kohl as a stand-in for the Reichstag dome by Sir Norman Foster. The dome was seen by critics as a bombastic gesture.

Richard Davies

51 Photo montage of renovated Reichstag. The compromise dome shown here, prior to a last-minute alteration, was likened by German politicians to a camel's hump or an enormous night light.

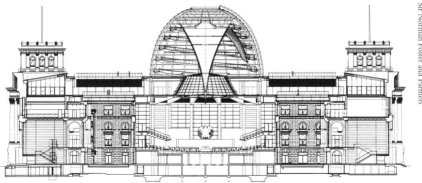

Sir Norman Foster and Partners

52 Section of final design for Reichstag renovation. The building's dome conceals a reflective glass cylinder to illuminate the plenary chamber with natural light and also provide natural ventilation.

53 Addition to German Historical Museum designed by I. M. Pei (left) and former Prussian Royal Arsenal (right), now housing the main part of the historical museum.

54 Model of addition showing glass-enclosed lobby. Chancellor Helmut Kohl personally hired Pei to create a modern annex to this "temple of Prussian militarism."

55 Model showing Pei's triangular addition to German Historical Museum next to the square neoclassical former Prussian Royal Arsenal. "Into this melancholy, deeply tragic place . . . [Pei] brings Americanism, world culture, and civilization."

56 Model of Pei's renovation of courtyard in former Prussian Royal Arsenal showing convex glass roof. Pei clashed with landmark preservation officials over plans to install trees and clear the courtyard of dozens of cannons to ensure a relaxing ambience.

57 Neue Wache, Prussian Royal Guardhouse designed by Karl Friedrich Schinkel and completed in
    1818. The interior was refurbished as unified Germany's Central Memorial to Victims of War and
    Tyranny in 1993.

58 Statue by Käthe Kollwitz installed in the Neue Wache in 1993. It was criticized as a Christian sym-
    bol unsuitable to memorialize Jewish Holocaust victims.

Richard Gruber

Klaus J. Dobberke

Marga and Walter Prankl, Heribert Heere

Renata Stih and Frieder Schnock

59-62 A 1995 competition for a national memorial to Jewish Holocaust victims drew 528 entries—many gargantuan and often grotesque. When the models went on display, they were described as a "quarry for anthropologists" seeking to examine the condition of a confused nation.

Bernd Kuhnert

63 Rendering of competition-winning Memorial to the Murdered Jews of Europe, designed by artists' collective under the direction of Christine Jackob-Marks. Chancellor Kohl blocked execution of the project, which involved a concrete tombstone covering an area larger than a football field.

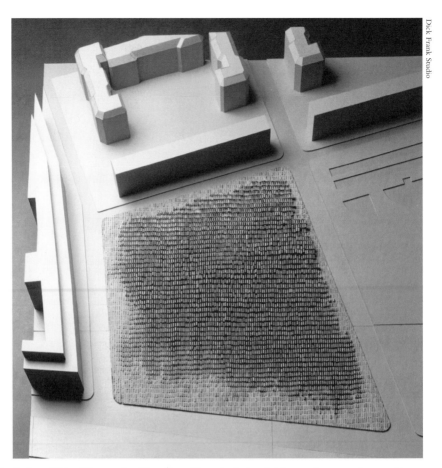

64 Sculptor Richard Serra and architect Peter Eisenman designed this entry in a second competition for a memorial to Jewish Holocaust victims. Its 4000 concrete slabs would be arrayed like a burial ground—or a bed of nails for the German national conscience.

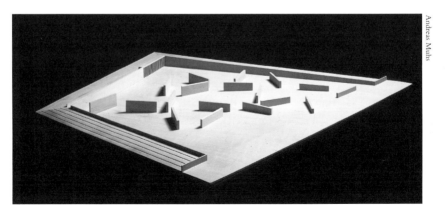

65 An entry by Berlin architect Gesine Weinmiller entailed an open plaza with eighteen walls of sandstone block scattered around the square. The jury praised it for resisting attempts to find redemptive meaning for the Holocaust in art and architecture.

grander visible sign that echoed Wallot's cupola. Foster tried to win them over with what he called a progressive new symbol, and experimented with dozens of cupolas, domes, and towers, projecting them onto the building like assorted wigs on a mannequin *(see figure 48)*. He argued that if he were obliged to raise the building's silhouette, a large glass cylinder, which he labeled a lighthouse of democracy, would be the best fit. The Social Democratic Party voted to support this option. But the flat circular element topping the cylinder earned it the nickname "flying saucer" among members of Chancellor Kohl's conservative Christian Democratic Union who relentlessly pushed for a dome. The liberal Free Democrats, the minority partner in the CDU-led government, wanted a modern rounded dome, while the small environmentalist Green Party saw no need for any elevated roof structure. Ultimately, the CDU realized that replicating Wallot's cupola would prove too expensive, and the modern rounded dome was approved by both the Building Committee and parliament's guiding Senior Council in June 1994 *(see figure 49)*.

Foster gave in to his clients' demand, and in the end no one seemed happy with the result. The proposed modern dome had the look of half an egg or a camel's hump until the architect made an eleventh-hour change to even out its geometry, making it rounder and more squat. At the very least it seemed certain to alleviate the original Reichstag's outward solemnity. The architectural journal *Bauwelt* published a caricature showing Chancellor Kohl's bald pate as a stand-in for the dome *(see figure 50)*, together with a commentary terming it a symbol by which Germans sought to declare a renewed greatness, a sense of being "somebody again."[192] But if this was a nationalist gesture, it appeared to be a half-hearted one. The dome born of political compromise prompted second thoughts even among parliamentarians who had previously supported it. "Actually, nobody wants the thing," said Building Committee Chairman Kansy.[193]

It was not the first awkward cupola politicians imposed onto a symbolic public building. In 1947, the modernist team designing the United Nations headquarters plopped an abstracted dome atop the UN General

Assembly to placate conservative members of the United States Congress for fear they might block funds for a domeless chamber.[194] The U.S. legislature's own history of dome disputes indicates perhaps that Foster's Reichstag crown may not be immune to still further modification in the long run. The Washington Capitol's original early-nineteenth-century wooden dome, designed by Charles Bulfinch, was ridiculed by some Americans as resembling an upside-down kettle or an overturned washbowl.[195] It was torn down and replaced within little over a quarter of a century by a more stately cast-iron framed dome, designed by Thomas Ustick Walter and completed in 1866, that came to symbolize for many the majesty and solidity of American democracy.

To counter objections from those who read any Reichstag dome as an authoritarian symbol, Foster did not leave it empty, but filled it with a pair of spiral viewing ramps intertwined in a double helix (see figure 52). Scheduled to be open to visitors even when the Bundestag is in session, the dome aimed to place the public above the politicians answerable to them. Searching to symbolically justify the design element he had previously opposed, Foster argued that the dome demonstrated a new beginning at the Reichstag and guided the country towards the future.[196]

Foster himself was every bit as interested in problem solving as declarative gestures. So he deftly turned the dome he never wanted into a tour de force of technological wizardry. Within its outer shell of twenty-four steel ribs embedded with Austrian-made glass panels, he concealed an enormous reflective glass cylinder to help illuminate the plenary chamber with indirect natural light and provide natural ventilation. The dome will also feature a massive retractable metal panel that rotates within the outer shell to block direct sunlight from creating unwanted glare and heat in the chamber. Foster introduced other energy-saving elements pleasing to Germany's environmentally conscious electorate. The most significant is a plan to make the building energy efficient through its own electrical power plant run by rapeseed oil, utilizing the exhaust heat from the combustion process for heating and cooling the parliament.[197] The dome will be further equipped with a built-in mechanical cleaning device to ensure a sparkling luster even in gritty Berlin's often inclement weather.

Gleaming high-tech elements will predominate inside the Reichstag, where the 1,200 ton dome will sit atop concrete pillars encircling the legislative chamber. A set of steel rods arrayed like spokes of a bicycle wheel within the circumference of the dome's base will resist the dome's outward thrust, simultaneously acting as a structural necessity and a decorative device.[198] Although Foster had originally proposed using the same circular seating arrangement that Behnisch deployed in Bonn, the parliamentarians rejected the round form after putting almost as much debate into the matter as into the question of the dome. Most were unhappy with the auditory qualities and sightlines in the Bonn chamber, so they opted for a three-quarter circle arrangement considered more conducive to debate. There will be 672 deputies when the inaugural session is held in the Foster-designed chamber. But this number will be reduced to 598 in the year 2002 as a result of a 1996 Bundestag vote to reorganize legislative districts. The Bundesrat, the far smaller upper chamber of parliament which reviews legislation passed by the policy-making Bundestag, decided only in September 1996 that it too would move to Berlin. It will base its 69 members in another refurbished Berlin building, the former Prussian House of Lords, erected in 1903. Hamburg architect Peter Schweger was put in charge of the renovation in 1997.

Foster tried to recapture the majesty of the interior spaces of the old Reichstag, severely toned down during Baumgarten's 1960s refurbishment when the main entrance was moved to the less prominent north facade of the building; Foster has shifted it back to the grand western portal with its six towering Corinthian columns (see figure 51). Visitors, who before unification came into the Reichstag as if sneaking in guiltily via the side door, now will mount Wallot's grand central steps as if ascending an acropolis and enter on axis to a soaring foyer. Foster also ordered restoration of the original Athenian proportions of Wallot's doorways, reduced under Baumgarten from almost eleven feet high to seven feet.

Under Foster, the 1960s modifications will disappear almost entirely. In the process of uncovering the sandstone walls beneath drywall facing, hundreds of graffiti messages left by the Red Army soldiers who helped conquer Nazism were revealed. "We came with the sword to Berlin in order to remove forever the sword from the hands of the Germans," wrote one soldier in a typical message.[199] Many of these Cyrillic scrawls—regiment members wrote with the charcoal remains of the Reichstag's burnt timber interior, officers used their blue map pencils—will be preserved. This step is noteworthy considering that it involves showcasing evidence of national defeat and humiliation while paying tribute to the now vanished Soviet power that removed fascism's yoke. But the value of saving all the graffiti came under challenge in 1996 when comprehensive translations were made available to the Bundestag courtesy of the Russian Embassy in Berlin. It turned out that though many Soviet soldiers left declarations of wartime patriotism and Slavic equivalents of "Kilroy was here," there were also lewd scribblings of the sort found on men's room walls. Preservationists argued that historical authenticity should override prudery. Foster pressed for conserving as many as possible, raw language or not. He also kept some old raw stone surfaces, including shell and bullet marks, along with openly exposed charred fragments, as additional reminders of the past rather than totally recladding or polishing the Reichstag's historic core anew.

In the end, it cost more to renovate the old Reichstag than to build an entirely new parliament building. It is by far the single most expensive state architectural project in unified Berlin, carrying a price tag of 600 million marks, or the 1997 equivalent of roughly 350 million dollars, nearly two-and-one-half times that of the Behnisch parliament completed in Bonn in 1992. Germany's Federal Auditing Office assailed the expense in a 1995 report and argued that 400 million marks should have sufficed.[200] Just how much of the German national treasury should be devoted to prestige architectural projects had been a source of earlier disgruntlement. In *Mein Kampf*, Hitler cited the sum spent on Wallot's design to support his complaint that Germany's expenditure on state buildings was "laughable and inadequate." While a single battleship cost approximately 60 million marks according to his calculations, Hitler complained that less than half that amount was appropriated for "the first magnificent building of the Reich, intended to stand for eternity, the Reichstag Building."[201]

The Bundestag's move into the renovated Reichstag will bring parliament and Germany at large back into physical contact with its history in a way the legislature managed to avoid for four decades by virtue of Bonn's modernity. Michael Cullen, the author of an authoritative history of the Reichstag who first suggested the idea of wrapping the Reichstag to Christo, has urged that the Bundestag decorate the restored Reichstag with artworks that reflect an awareness of its past, including portraits of German champions of democracy under both the Wilhelmine Empire and the Weimar Republic. "The tradition in the Schwippert building or in the Behnisch building may have been ahistorical, but the Reichstag Building demands the presence of the history of German parliamentarism and its most important representatives," Cullen argued.[202] The name by which the building will be known when it houses the Bundestag will further reflect historical consciousness. Under the Weimar Republic, even though parliament acquired expanded constitutional powers, Germans found it difficult to break with the customs of time past and continued to call its home the Reichstag. Until now, the imperial tag has stuck.

Foster's domed Reichstag represents a determined rupture with the subdued expression of German democratic power as conceived by postwar architects in Bonn, but retains its familiar modernist idiom of glazed transparency. More than a century after Wallot sought to display the character of a unified German state with a confused synthetic style, the Bundestag is getting a new home created by an architect who treats his profession much like a science or an industrial process. The question of forging a German national style that preoccupied the Reichstag's original designer never occurred to the British exemplar of technocratic prowess in a globalized culture. Clarity, computer-age craftsmanship, and industrial perfection rather than rhetorical flourishes are the prevailing characteristics of Foster's work. "High technology buildings are hand-crafted with the same care as bricks and mortar, or timber," Foster has written. "Hand-crafted care is the factor which makes a building loved by its users, and by those who look at it."[203] All the care and money going into the reborn Reichstag notwithstanding, the political history made in its restored premises will be a key determinant of whether it captures the affection of Germany and the world.

I. M. PEI AND A PRUSSIAN INHERITANCE

Architectural remnants from the Nazi regime were not the only state buildings that presented a symbolic quandary in postwar Berlin. Along with Hitler's Reich Chancellery, the World War II allies considered destroying the centuries-old Zeughaus, the former Royal Arsenal, because they regarded it as the embodiment of the German militarist tradition that culminated in Nazi aggression. This massive baroque quadrangle was encrusted with bellicose imagery celebrating the victories of Prussia, the entity that went on to lead the empire after the unification of German states in 1871. "If the Allies have any sense," the American correspondent William L. Shirer wrote upon seeing the ravaged arsenal soon after the conquest of Nazi Berlin, "they will blow the remains of it up to help the Germans forget it."[204] The Allies formally abolished Prussia in 1947, but they ultimately decided against razing its arsenal while stipulating that the "Zeughaus be fully stripped of its previous character and be put into service as a symbolic place for the peaceful reconstruction of Berlin."[205]

The arsenal's location near the Hohenzollern Royal Palace along Unter den Linden put it within the Soviet-controlled sector of East Berlin. Hundreds of bronze cannon previously stored there were melted down or scrapped on orders of the Soviet military command. Despite the building's incongruous iconography, the self-professed "peace-loving" German Democratic Republic revamped the arsenal in the early 1950s for use as a museum of Marxist-Leninist history, where exhibits included a portion of the old Zeughaus military collection returned to the East Germans by the Soviet Union.

But if the building no longer served chiefly as a storehouse for the tools of war, it was hardly stripped of its symbolic decorations. Even now, triumphant war deities figure among the forty-four sculptures adorning the cornice. Mars looms atop a pair of enchained slaves, and his wife, the goddess Bellona, stands with an outstretched sword atop a pile of booty. A relief on the pediment shows Minerva teaching battle technique. Carved stone military helmets embellish the keystones set above the windows of the building that was designed largely by Johann Arnold Nering and Jean de Bodt. A Latin inscription over the main entrance proclaims, "To terrify the enemy with his righteous armament and to protect his people and allies, Frederick 1, King of Prussia, built this arsenal in 1706 and filled it with weapons, booty, and trophies of all sorts."[206]

Rational thought and cultural achievement also figured prominently in the Prussian tradition, but it was authoritarian Prussia's military prowess that most appealed to the Nazis. They drew readily upon this heritage to bolster their own armed conquests of Europe. Recognizing the potential of remembered grandeur to move his followers, Hitler took care to kindle the embers of Prussian glory in official ceremonies and state rituals. His propaganda chief Joseph Goebbels declared, "The character of National Socialism is Prussian, and the character of Prussianness is National Socialist."[207] For much of World War II, Nazi exhibitions urging valor and bravery by German soldiers and the citizenry at large were staged in the Zeughaus's expansive halls. Hitler and other high-level Nazi leaders presided over parades and commemorative events in its courtyard.

When Berlin was still divided in the mid-1980s, Chancellor Kohl decided that the Federal Republic should build its own German Historical Museum in the Western sector of the city to help West German citizens shore up what Kohl and others saw as a weak sense of German historical identity. The Italian architect Aldo Rossi created a lavish design. Ground was broken for the project in October 1987, and Kohl declared, "We can do justice neither to the past nor to future generations if we do not know from where we come, if we do not know the history of our people and do not remind ourselves of it—in its heights and in its depths."[208] Unification and the transfer of the capital from Bonn thwarted realization of the Rossi plan, in part because of its high cost and the fact it was to be located on the Spreebogen site now designated by the chancellor for his own office. Just as the ministries moving to Berlin from Bonn had to make do with existing buildings rather than construct new structures, Kohl's museum ended up inheriting the arsenal as its quarters.

The director of the German Historical Museum, Christoph Stölzl, would have much preferred to locate it in a modern home unencumbered by martial connotations. In fact, the original guidelines by the museum's founding commission stressed the symbolic necessity of housing it in a new building. "The commission stated clearly, 'Please, no historicizing architecture for a German Historical Museum,'" Stölzl said. Yet, not only did the museum end up with antiquated state-built architecture, but a building that the director calls "the temple of Prussian militarism."[209]

Once Stölzl had dismantled the musty Marxist dioramas and other communist-era showpieces that filled the arsenal under the East Germans, he installed a permanent exhibition that aimed to place German history in a larger European context. The exhibit's story line serves to buttress the Kohl government's commitment to the European Union, although the museum director admitted that it stood at odds with its location in a building that celebrates Prussia's victories over its European neighbors.[210] To counterbalance the "temple of Prussian militarism," Kohl has commissioned a thoroughly modern annex potentially more conducive to the museum's current message *(see figure 53)*. As with the Reichstag overhaul by Sir Norman Foster, Germany sought the aid of a foreign star architect to deal with an awkward national monument. But while the Bundestag held an open competition to renovate its Berlin home, Kohl acted single-handedly in choosing the Chinese-American I. M. Pei, who added the glass pyramid to the Louvre in Paris and designed the East Wing of the National Gallery of Art in Washington, D.C. "The new museum is trying to do something that the Zeughaus can no longer do," said Pei. "It is for changing exhibitions that will tell the story of the history of Germany in a way that the Zeughaus is not capable of doing, because it will bring about a certain sort of biased point of view about Germany. Stölzl feels that the story can never be told properly there."[211]

Perhaps Kohl envied French President François Mitterrand's ease in setting his mark on his own capital with the building of the Grands Projets. A postwar German leader could enjoy no such leeway. The chancellor's failure to hold an open design competition for the museum job was pounced upon by Berlin's Senator for Urban Development Peter Strieder as "smacking of monarchism."[212] Already, the chancellor had come under attack from leftist politicians and intellectuals who distrusted the motives behind his museum plan. "History does not belong to the government," said Social Democratic politician Freimut Duve in 1986. "Nor does it belong to politics. In a democracy the government neither can nor should be building museums in the manner of feudal lords in the olden days."[213]

Kohl's involvement in planning Berlin's redesign has come nowhere close to rivaling Mitterrand's near autocratic interventions in changing the face of the French capital with additions to the Louvre and several other cultural projects. Kohl, as Pei recounted about his meetings with the chancellor, made no pretense of being knowledgeable about architecture and communicated no definitive vision for the German Historical Museum Annex. With the design of the Louvre extension, by contrast, "Mitterrand was involved with the big idea but also with the details," Pei said. The French president insisted on personally inspecting the materials that were used throughout the Louvre pyramid, from the glass panels of its surface, to the stainless steel trusses that supported them, to the stone used in the capacious entry lobby beneath. "He asked to see everything," the architect added. "I don't think I would expect that from Mr. Kohl. Maybe, but I don't think so. They are two very different people. To begin with, Mitterrand was a very cultivated person. I'm not saying that Kohl is not. Kohl is obviously a person who was brought up in a very different way. Mitterrand, like all French presidents, had the grandeur of France built into him. I don't believe that kind of feeling of grandeur is in Kohl.

Kohl is a very simple and easy-to-understand person."[214] According to Pei, the disparities between the two men were as much a matter of national histories and cultures as they were of divergent personalities.

At the Louvre, Pei proved himself adept at grafting a contemporary crystalline design onto a classical stone-faced landmark. At the German Historical Museum, the celebrated architect displays another characteristic—the tasteful blandness that has earned him great favor as a purveyor of restrained modernism to establishment clients. His less successful projects, like the John F. Kennedy Library outside Boston in Dorchester, Massachusetts and the Rock and Roll Hall of Fame and Museum in Cleveland, are banal vessels composed of recycled geometric forms and truss-supported glass facades.

The design of the Historical Museum Annex risks falling into the same category. It will have a large curved glass facade with a spiral staircase encased in a transparent glass cylinder *(see figure 54)*, ill-suited to its setting alongside either the baroque exuberance of the Zeughaus or the ordered clarity of two nearby neoclassical buildings designed by Karl Friedrich Schinkel, the Neue Wache (New Guardhouse) and the Altes Museum. "It has to be itself, to be very simple, and to be very honest," Pei said. "I made no attempt to try and say, 'Come look at me,' or to say, 'I'm part of German history.' I made no attempt because I would not succeed."[215]

The four-story annex will be located on a heretofore isolated site behind the Zeughaus and the Neue Wache, a nineteenth-century cubic structure built for Prussian royal guardsmen that now serves as Germany's main national war memorial. That memorial stands across from another, more subtle monument commemorating the 1933 Nazi burnings of "un-German" books. "He enlivens the area," Stölzl enthused about Pei's annex design. "Into this melancholy, deeply tragic place, he brings Americanism, world culture, and civilization."[216] The annex will give a new prominence to the spot, turning it into a pedestrian throughway linked with the cluster of art museums that occupy Museum Island to the north of Unter den Linden.

Visitors circulating within Pei's glass-enclosed atrium, to be illumi-
nated at night like a giant lantern, will have a direct view of the north
facade of the arsenal. Ascending its spiral staircase they will be able to ogle
the sculptural program that discomfited the World War II allies and still
gives momentary pause to Stölzl. But late-twentieth-century museum-
goers are more likely to associate warfare with supersonic jets and nuclear
missiles than statues of mythological deities, however aggressive their
depiction. From the vantage point of today's visitor to Pei's building, the
military propaganda of centuries past will be transmuted into art historical treasures.

Pei is still not satisfied that his design completes the arsenal's mutation
and aims to remove at least part of the building's remaining military heritage to better suit the museum's contemporary needs. He has been asked
to redesign—in addition to the annex commission—the arsenal's courtyard
as a year-round cafe *(see figures 55 and 56)*. Pei proposed re-covering it with
a convex glass roof to replace that which sat atop the courtyard from 1877
until its destruction in World War II. Pei also plans to fill the courtyard
with ficus trees and jazz music. To ensure a relaxing ambiance he wants to
remove dozens of cannons that are currently arrayed around all four sides
of the court, their barrels aimed towards the center. "The cannons are not
sympathetic," Pei said. "I don't want to sit down and have a cup of coffee
and look at cannons. . . . I want to humanize the building. I want to soft-
en the image of the building."[217]

His way of doing that—by creating the sort of heavily trafficked atrium that has become commonplace in cultural and commercial centers
around the globe—has justifiably dismayed some Germans. "I know
German friends may not agree with me," Pei conceded. "They might say
I'm bringing American kitsch here." Berlin landmark officials are opposed
to the ahistorical installation of greenery and the removal of cannons that
have been part and parcel of the arsenal since its foundation three centuries ago. Even if Pei were to have his way, attentive cafe patrons may be
disturbed by a more immutable architectural element—the twenty-two

agonized faces of dying soldiers carved into the keystones around the interior court. These, like the helmets on the outer facade, were designed by Andreas Schlüter in the 1690s and present an unsettling counterpoint to the triumphal decorations on the exterior. Contorted in pain and despair, the faces have been variously interpreted as attempts to frighten any enemies who might capture the building or as a means of reminding the Prussians themselves of the suffering inflicted by war. A critic for the daily *Süddeutsche Zeitung* charged that Pei's treatment of the courtyard "made a mockery" of its sculpted images. "To smother them with mood music would be tasteless. Even at the start of a new millennium, one would expect some degree of propriety towards history by a historical museum."[218]

In the new millennium's freewheeling multimedia climate, Pei's modern design will forego the explicitly didactic pretensions of a building like the Prussian Royal Arsenal, dating from an era when the state had a tighter grip on cultural expression and monumental architecture perhaps had greater popular resonance. Nonetheless, at a national museum devoted to interpreting and presenting history, even an architecture of empty abstraction can be enlisted as an image-making tool.

MEMORY IN THE NEW BERLIN

As Berlin undergoes regeneration, many awkward physical reminders of its past are beginning to disappear. Increasingly, fresh plaster covers the pockmarks left by bullets and bomb blasts, new construction plugs gaps emptied by war-time destruction, and the one-hundred-mile-long Wall that divided the city for close to three decades has all but vanished. Coinciding with the removal of wounds to the urban landscape are efforts to focus the commemoration of history on specific sites by creating national memorials. Memory, of course, has been at the heart of Germany's capital dilemma. The vexing issue of commemoration versus forgetting has been played out in both the city's new architectural projects and decisions about whether and how to preserve its older buildings.

In early 1993, Chancellor Kohl obtained government approval for renovating Berlin's Neue Wache, the former Prussian Royal Guardhouse on Unter den Linden, and designating it as unified Germany's "Central Memorial to the Victims of War and Tyranny" *(see figure 57)*. Other nations had memorials to their fallen, Kohl said, and called it a question of "our country's dignity" for Germany to have one as well.[219] During a Bundestag debate over the Neue Wache's restoration, the chancellor assailed what he considered Germany's lack of a sufficiently worthy site where foreign dignitaries could observe international protocol and lay wreaths while paying state visits to Bonn.

In 1964 at Bonn's university grounds, West German President Heinrich Lübke had dedicated a small monument to the war dead that could be visited by foreign leaders. Consisting of a crucifix and a bronze plaque, it was in line with other aspects of the unusual capital in not calling attention to itself—a far cry from the Cenotaph in London designed by Sir Edwin Lutyens and inscribed "To the Glorious Dead" or the tombs of unknown soldiers at Arlington National Cemetery outside Washington, D.C. and under the Arc de Triomphe in Paris. Repeated attempts to create a more prominent monument in Bonn came to naught. The efforts foundered on intense opposition, mainly from descendants of members of the anti-Nazi resistance movement who argued that such a memorial could not be realized if it lumped ss members together with resistance fighters and Jews killed in gas chambers. The Green Party went so far as to posit the futility of creating any German national war memorial. "State guests from abroad who want to honor the dead by laying a wreath or other gestures," stated the Greens' parliamentary fraction, "will understand that in the Federal Republic of Germany the erection of a national monument will run aground because of the danger of equating the deaths of perpetrators and victims of National Socialist crimes against humanity."[220]

Kohl blurred the distinction in 1985 by successfully pressuring U.S. President Ronald Reagan to accompany him on a visit to the military cemetery of Bitburg, where Waffen-ss troops lay buried, only hours after the two leaders paid homage to those who perished at Bergen-Belsen. In unified Berlin, too, Kohl brushed aside protests about commemorating the totality of war dead in one place. For that purpose, he took charge of a plan to redo the inside of the Neue Wache, a templelike neoclassical structure designed by Schinkel. Kohl exacerbated controversy by choosing as the memorial's focal point a Käthe Kollwitz sculpture of a mother cradling her dead son, a pietà *(see figure 58)*. He saw the bronze statue as a readily comprehensible image, but critics viewed this Christian symbol as highly unsuitable if Jewish Holocaust victims were presumed to figure among those being memorialized. Only at the insistence of leaders of minority groups within German society were bronze plaques specifically listing Jewish, Gypsy, and homosexual victims of Nazism hastily erected under the building's Doric portico. The refurbished guardhouse, which had previously served as a national memorial under both the Nazis and the Communists, has not surprisingly failed to gain widespread acceptance as a commemorative spot after reopening to the public in November 1993. Tourists wandering down Unter den Linden peek in out of curiosity, but many Germans feel the need to look elsewhere to perform acts of remembrance.

Hard on the heels of the Neue Wache rededication came bitter infighting over a separate plan to build a major Berlin memorial specifically devoted to Jewish victims of the Holocaust. The project originated a year before the Berlin Wall came down, in 1988, and went on to assume heightened significance after unification. It was spearheaded by a prominent television journalist named Lea Rosh who organized an umbrella organization of intellectuals, cultural figures, and civic and business leaders to raise private funds for the memorial's construction. The group initially envisioned a monument, formally called the "Memorial to the Murdered Jews of Europe," on or near the site of the former Gestapo Headquarters.

The memorial's significance grew exponentially when Berlin's halves were rejoined and efforts began to transform the city into the government seat. National politicians saw the memorial as an important symbolic and urbanistic component of the new capital, prompting the federal government to donate a more prominent plot that would cover an entire city block just south of the Brandenburg Gate. Prior to unification, this site fell within the no-man's-land adjacent to the Wall. It also stood near the location of the bunker where Hitler spent his final hours before killing himself as Soviet troops closed in on Berlin. The actual site of the bunker itself was unavailable, having been blanketed over in the early 1980s by a set of East German apartment towers and a kindergarten.

"Until now, there has been no central monument in the land of the perpetrators that recalls and warns about the deed," argued a brochure produced by the monument's backers. Their call for a monument was well motivated, even if they gave less than adequate consideration to how a Holocaust memorial in Berlin might differ from one in Washington or Jerusalem. Conceptually and aesthetically, the Berlin project poses singular demands since one might expect that a German-built memorial will express shame as well as sorrow. Furthermore, in the land of the perpetrators, evidence of the crime itself is readily at hand. Located in Berlin and its environs are the Gestapo Headquarters, the villa where the Wannsee Conference was held to coordinate the "final solution," and the Sachsenhausen concentration camp, as well as places where opponents of Nazi rule were executed.

While funds fell short for upkeep at these older sites, millions of dollars were to be spent on a new, single, centralized memorial. Ironically, then, its creation might actually facilitate the process of forgetting, argued the directors of museums and memorials at former concentration camps in Germany. A group of those who oversaw the deteriorating remains of Buchenwald, Dachau, Sachsenhausen, and Bergen-Belsen feared that the Berlin monument could endanger "concrete confrontation" with the past at the very sites where it occurred.[221] The directors argued that a commitment to arduous task of preservation would be a more fitting way to bear witness for future generations.

The planned national memorial came under further attack from cynical Berliners who derided it as a "wreath dumping place," or *Kranzabwurfstelle*. There, public figures could fulfill protocol and lay garlands as Kohl desired, but this merely entailed providing a venue for perfunctory ceremonies without rigorous confrontation with the legacy of the past. Others feared that a state-sponsored memorial solely for Jews would lead to a "hierarchy of victims" and risk echoing the Nazis' own racial selection process. Additional campaigns, led by Germany's Union of Gays and the Central Council of Sinti and Roma, were begun to promote the erection of national memorials in Berlin to the homosexuals and Gypsies who died at the hands of the Nazis.

Throughout the early 1990s, Rosh pressed forward, undeterred by these objections, though they would continue to arise with growing vehemence. Together with the federal government and Berlin city authorities, her group sponsored a design competition for the proposed memorial. It attracted 528 entries, including twelve by invitation from internationally recognized artists, among them Richard Serra, Rebecca Horn, Dani Karavan, and Christian Boltanski. The results highlighted the perils of aesthetic representations of the Holocaust.

The competition's guidelines advised participants that they had five acres at their disposal. Most entrants were determined to use it all. The designs they submitted were gargantuan and often grotesque, reflecting an apparent belief that the extraordinary dimensions of Nazi crimes necessitated a monument of equal magnitude. One artist, Richard Gruber, proposed an immense Ferris wheel equipped not with compartments for thrill-seekers but with sixteen freight cars like those in which Jews were transported to the death camps *(see figure 59)*. Gruber wrote in an accompanying text that he envisioned the rotating monument as a demonstration of the "tension between hope and hopelessness, between a carnival and genocide."[222] A separate proposal envisioned a sixty-foot high oven, modeled on those used at death camps, that would burn round-the-clock; another called for erecting a container 130 feet tall and 100 feet wide as a symbolic vessel for the blood of the six million.

Replicating the Temple of Solomon on the monument site or constructing various types of massive Jewish stars there also figured among the entries *(see figures 60 and 61)*. One of the stars of David would be crowned by a broken heart connoting German remorse over the killing of its Jewish population; another would be landscaped with yellow petaled perennials to evoke the badge Nazis forced Jews to wear. The potential use of these emblems by the contemporary German state seemed bizarre or at the very least inappropriate. When the extraordinary array of design submissions went on public view for two weeks in the former Council of State Building in 1995, author Henryk Broder described it as "a quarry for anthropologists, psychologists, and behaviorists" interested in examining the "condition of a confused nation that wants to create a monument to its victims in order to purify itself."[223]

A few entries stood out in radical contrast, having been submitted in protest against the organizers' perceived need for monumental symbolism.

One such entry urged building a bus stop on the memorial grounds from which public transport would be available for those wanting to visit the former concentration camps *(see figure 62)*. The concept, presented by Renata Stih and Frieder Schnock, sought to refocus attention on the sites within Germany where mass murder was implemented. Another advocate of this sort of "counter-monument," Horst Hoheisel of Kassel, proposed that the Brandenburg Gate be ground to dust and strewn around the memorial grounds in a gesture by which Germany would sacrifice the landmark archway in penance for the murder of European Jewry. The empty place in the urban landscape would recall the Jews' absence. Of course, such proposals had little chance of success, but in the end they did influence the country's thinking about the memorial and its objectives.

The winning entry fulfilled the worst nightmares of detractors fearful that the memorial would be exploited as a way to bury the past. It was a concrete tombstone twenty-three feet thick and covering almost the entire block, an area larger than a football field *(see figure 63)*. Set at an incline, it would be inscribed with the names of all known Jewish Holocaust victims. The design, by a Berlin artists' collective under the direction of Christine Jackob-Marks, also called for a variant on the Jewish custom in which the living honor the dead by placing small stones atop grave markers. In this case, the stones were to be eighteen boulders, brought to the site from Masada in Israel, the last outpost of Jewish zealots battling against Roman conquerors in the first century B.C.

The leader of today's community of Jews in Germany, Ignatz Bubis, immediately voiced reservations about erecting such a large national cenotaph, an empty tomb for those whose remains lie elsewhere. Bubis felt its exhaustive list of the murdered would actually heighten the victims' anonymity rather than personalize their fate and perpetuate their memory. "The name of Moses Rabbinowitch would appear a thousand times," he said.[224] Further complicating fulfillment of the artists' concept was the fact that the names of over a million Jews from Eastern Europe had never been documented. Once such a prominent Jewish figure as

Bubis had expressed his qualms, German politicians, who had until then shied away from criticizing the project for fear of making a misstep, felt less reluctant to air their misgivings. Kohl and Berlin Mayor Eberhard Diepgen, alarmed at the prospect of the monument's funerary shadow hanging in perpetuity over the heart of the revived capital, criticized the scale of the winning entry, thereby creating a stalemate and effectively putting its construction on hold.

Dozens of German politicians and cultural figures—with the exception of Rosh, who stood firm in her support for the megatombstone—criticized the design in a series of three officially organized symposia on the monument project. The symposia, held in early 1997, made it clear that the debate about the monument was not simply a discussion about aesthetics or urban design. Like all the state architectural projects for the capital, the memorial proved Germany's self-definition and historical understanding were also at stake. Not only the built form of the proposed monument came under scrutiny during these discussions but also the degree to which it could and should express collective national responsibility for the Nazi crimes.

The symposia came shortly after Harvard political scientist Daniel Jonah Goldhagen's book, *Hitler's Willing Executioners: Ordinary Germans and the Holocaust*, became a best-seller in Germany. Goldhagen's central argument—that a deep strain of popular German anti-Semitism led up to mass murder and turned the extermination of the Jews into a national project—resonated in the remarks of many participants. Berlin historian Hans-Ernst Mittig worried that placing the memorial in proximity to the former site of Hitler's Reich Chancellery ran the risk of assigning guilt for the genocide too closely to a single personality. Others argued that erecting the memorial in just this location was akin to trying to drive a stake through the heart of a vampire to kill it once and for all. Alternatively, several participants proposed that placing the memorial closer to contemporary democratic state institutions like the Parliament and the Chancellery would better demonstrate Germany's commitment to enduring recognition of its responsibility for the Holocaust. They suggested the Platz der Republik, directly opposite the Bundestag's new home in the former Reichstag Building. Rosh countered that it was not the German people at large who carried out the murders, and that by placing the monument in front of the Reichstag, one came dangerously close to erroneously asserting collective guilt.

As the months passed and work on construction of the unified capital began to alter the skyline, the city and federal government linked the memorial's realization to the timing of the government transfer from Bonn. They were intent on getting the project built along with the completion of the major capital structures, and set as a groundbreaking deadline January 20, 1999, the anniversary of the 1942 Wannsee Conference at which German officials met to coordinate the mass murder of European Jewry. But in view of the widespread dissatisfaction voiced after the 1995 competition, they agreed to have a new round of artists, including those top-listed in the original contest, submit new or revised designs. The guidelines for this second attempt were more carefully defined than the first and aimed to avoid another crop of gargantuan entries by stating that more important than the monument's size was how it fit into the urban context. Many of those invited, including James Turrell and Rachel Whiteread, were minimalists skeptical of nineteenth-century monumentality's ongoing relevance and efficacy.

To assist in the second memorial competition, the Germans turned to an American professor of English and Judaic studies, James E. Young, who wrote an insightful survey of Holocaust memorials but had never before served on an architectural jury. Young accepted an official invitation to join a panel of four distinguished German architects and art historians in reviewing the invited entries. Like other foreigners asked to weigh designs for Berlin capital projects, Young was astounded at the Germans' lack of faith in their own judgment. Once deliberations got under way, he said, "They began by asking me, 'What do make of this?' They began deferring to me more and more." Young's Jewishness probably played a role. "They didn't know anything from Jewish. They had no idea how any of these designs would fit or not fit" as appropriate iconography for a memorial to Jewish victims.[225]

In November 1997, four designs—by conceptual artist Jochen Gerz, by architect Daniel Libeskind, by architect Gesine Weinmiller, and by sculptor Richard Serra working together with architect Peter Eisenman—were chosen from a group of nineteen. The four had a simplicity and an aesthetic rigor lacking in most submissions to the original competition.

Particularly sobering was the Serra-Eisenman scheme, which consisted of 4,000 concrete slabs arrayed like a vast burial ground or an undulating bed of nails for the German national conscience (see figure 64). But this kind of memorial, designed by two well-known Jewish Americans, had the same drawback as Jackob-Marks's concrete tombstone in that both covered the entire site, their inhuman proportions in keeping with the hugeness of the crime. Moreover, it seemed likely to inject a permanently menacing element into the capital city that would be unacceptable to some Germans. Others thought it imperative to create just such an open wound in central Berlin to keep the memory of Nazi atrocities alive. After Chancellor Kohl personally inspected a model of the Serra-Eisenman scheme, he expressed interest in its possible realization, while voicing uneasiness about its size and the lack of landscaping around its perimeter.

Weinmiller's proposal had a lighter touch, entailing an open plaza with eighteen walls of sandstone blocks scattered around the square (see figure 65). The seemingly random placement of the walls was meant to abstractly recall European Jewry's destruction. At the same time, it would create a fleeting perspectival illusion of a recomposed Star of David in the mind's eye of visitors to the site. The jury praised the design for resisting any attempt to find redemptive meaning for the Holocaust in art or architecture. Weinmiller herself, a thirty-five-year-old Berlin architect, was described as "a young German woman of the generation now obligated to shoulder the memory and shame of events for which she is not to blame."[226]

Whichever design is ultimately built, the contentious debate over the national memorial to Jewish Holocaust victims demonstrates that the public discussion of German responsibility for the past is by no means at an end and remains an unavoidable priority for most Germans. But if a memorial's purpose is to be an antidote to forgetting, a means of ensuring continuous engagement with the Holocaust and its moral imperatives, perhaps the debate itself was far more effective than any physical monument. "For it may be the finished monument that suggests an end to memory itself, puts a cap on memory-work, and draws a bottom line underneath an era that must always haunt Germany," advised Young. "Better a thousand years of Holocaust memorial competitions in Germany than any single 'final solution' to Germany's memorial problem."[227]

One could argue similarly about the country's capital dilemma and the anguished self-examination that Berlin's reinvention has provoked among German planners and politicians. Diplomats and political scientists will doubtless focus on a wealth of other factors in determining whither unified Germany, but the planning of the new Berlin remains a compelling gauge of the uncertain state of the nation. The capital's official face, which formerly proclaimed the might and merit of Prussia, Bismarck's empire, the Third Reich, and the dictatorship of the proletariat, is now becoming a vibrant architectural patchwork. It includes the renovation and reoccupation of structures dating from all of these bygone eras, as well as the addition of bold symbolic gestures like Foster's rebuilt Reichstag and Schultes's Chancellery. It unites approachable new and forbidding old architecture, buildings that embody the zeniths and nadirs of modern German history. Remarkably, these costly construction projects are to be juxtaposed not with freshly cast monuments to Germany's heroes but with a planned memorial at the restored capital's very heart to the victims of its worst crimes.

The new Berlin is less exuberant, experimental, and expansive than the unified German capital of which some had dreamed, and which others had dreaded. In contrast to Bonn, where an interim capital arose on a blank slate free of yesterday's traumas, Germany's latest national head-quarters grows on well-trodden, bloodied ground. By fitting the government structures into the city's existing fabric and empty terrain, instead of building entirely anew after erasing the architectural layers of previous political systems, Germany is proving a degree of willingness to live with its uncomfortable history rather than opting to repress it. And despite the nationalist euphoria that erupted soon after unification, the official architecture of the capital emerging thus far is neither triumphant nor encoded with assertions of postwar moral absolution.

For better or worse, the capital architecture also mirrors unified Germany's tendency to vacillate between forceful projections of its power and a reluctance to display its might on the world stage. On the one hand, the Germans have called the shots on European economic integration—sometimes to the dismay of their fellow Europeans—and on the other, they have been highly reluctant to exercise foreign policy leadership within the European Union. Even though it has the potential to exert influence over just about every sphere of European life, the new, larger Germany displays an almost obsessive degree of caution amid a struggle to moderate gestures of national aggrandizement.

The deeply ingrained collective memory of past aggression that shapes German actions in diplomatic and military realms has unquestionably affected the look of the new capital. The mixed signals sent by the latest capital architecture evince unified Germany's murky self-understanding and insecurity about its future direction. Blueprints mutated as

politicians' anxious calibration of architectural firepower turned into pre-
varication over built symbolism, an equivocation stemming from the
enduring eagerness of German officials to prove that their country is a
mature and reliable international partner. "We have only rarely in our history been able to find an answer to the question of who we really are,"
said Bundestag Vice President Hans Klein of the plans for Berlin. "When
we entered NATO in the fifties, there was the amusing saying, 'We must be
weaker than Luxembourg, but stronger than the Soviet Union,' and
between these poles, the postwar mentality has developed. It continually
expresses itself in childish ostentation on the one hand and a terribly
expensive affected modesty on the other."[228]

Nonetheless, those who desired a grander capital than Bonn have
also unmistakably shaped Berlin's recreation. Berlin has seen a shift from
the restrained architectural ambitions of the compact Rhineland town, as
well as a clear break with the styles embraced under Communist rule. If
Bonn's buildings exude a sense of atonement—an architectural hair shirt
for a contrite nation—Berlin has a different air simply because of its
grander, preexisting scale. At the same time, each new Berlin project was
born in a restricted budgetary climate resulting from the enormous
expense of revamping the bankrupt former East German economy and
infrastructure.

Whatever path they followed in designing Berlin's architectural and
urban structure, the Germans would have found their decisions contest-
ed. The engagement of high-visibility outsiders like Sir Norman Foster
and I. M. Pei was, in part, an attempt to circumvent this. Other foreign
architects gazing upon the myriad construction cranes over the city's
sandy soil have often voiced disappointment over what has arisen so far.
When the Union of International Architects held its annual convention
there in 1996, the union's President Rod Hackney assailed a lack of
German self-confidence and courage mirrored in the city's architecture.[229] "The Germans today are timid," Philip Johnson told another
Berlin gathering. "The Germans have made no great plans."[230] Aldo

Rossi reached a similar conclusion, saying, "I fear that Berlin has lost awareness of its destiny as a capital and in history."[231]

Architects like these have their own personal and professional agendas, and happily the Germans are creating a capital more consonant with Chancellor Helmut Kohl's commitment to furthering a European Germany instead of a German Europe. The degree to which Germany can live up to the ambitious commitments Kohl has made to European unification remains an open question. But because of Germany's federated structure, Berlin will not be the sole locus of power. In addition to the ministries staying behind in Bonn, the chancellor, the president, and the majority of government agencies moving to Berlin will retain liaison offices in Bonn as well. The central bank will remain in Frankfurt and is now scheduled to be subsumed within the new European Central Bank based in the same city. Germany's high court will stay in Karlsruhe, and the Federal Crime Agency, the equivalent of the FBI, will keep its headquarters in Wiesbaden. Berlin is on the way to becoming a capital of the kind of polycentric republic corresponding to an age when national decisions are often taken in consultation with other European Union countries, and ministers conduct their work today in Berlin, tomorrow in London, and the next in Madrid.

While working in Berlin, these ministers will find that Bonn's architecture of reticence has yet to be replaced by a clear-cut restatement of the national self-definition. Yes, the helter-skelter arrangement of Bonn has been abandoned in favor of clearly delineated urban design in keeping with Berlin tradition, but the Bonn design credo according to which buildings with "transparent" facades are the most appropriate homes to democratic institutions continues to hold many officials and architects in its thrall.

Not to be ignored are the younger German architects, like the team that designed the new Presidential Office and those who created the runner-up competition entry for the new Chancellery. They have a different reading of the democratic architectural symbols that gained currency in Bonn. The architectural solutions they proposed—but were unable to build as originally drafted—express a wish by at least some members of a new generation for fewer constraints in the design of a national image. This desire is likely to increase as World War II recedes further into the past, perhaps bringing with it changes in political culture and understanding of history.

The younger architects understandably decry a direct equivalency between a glass-enclosed parliament and government openness and accessibility. Less inhibition and a greater willingness to experiment could provide more compelling designs. Already with his new Chancellery, Axel Schultes is attempting to devise fresh imagery for a liberal democratic state. Such ongoing emphasis by Germans on the importance of architectural symbolism—their search for an architecture of democracy and a resolution to their capital dilemma—does matter since it arises not just from preternatural anxiety but also from a genuine desire to avoid past mistakes.

When Hans Schwippert designed the austere new Bundestag in Bonn half a century ago, he was firm in his refusal to elevate the stature of German public servants through a grand official architecture. That, he insisted, could come only "when politics again attains exalted levels."[232] "Exalted" may not be an entirely apt description of the German polity in the late 1990s, but the Federal Republic has made an exemplary transition from totalitarian rule to democracy. With this record in tow, a hesitant nation trades its modest Bonn base for a far more visible civic arena where, for years to come, the Germans are destined to weigh pride and assertiveness against the competing claim of responsibility for the past.

ACKNOWLEDGMENTS

The American Council on Germany, through its John J. McCloy Fellowships, enabled me to travel throughout Germany to interview government officials, planners, and architects about the country's built image. The Einstein Forum in Potsdam, under the direction of Gary Smith, provided additional support for research that led to this book.

Access to collections and periodicals at several libraries was indispensable, including the architectural library at the Technische Universität in Berlin, Avery Architectural and Fine Arts Library at Columbia University in New York, the Goethe House Library in New York, and the New York Public Library Center for the Humanities. I also owe thanks to Hannelore Koehler and John Alba at the German Information Center in New York.

Alexander Hass, Dagmar Rose, Tillmann Pinder, Fanny Hass, and Gabriele Hass gave me friendship, bountiful hospitality, and a home away from home in Berlin.

In addition to those whose interviews are cited in these pages, many people shared thoughts and advice, including Stefan Braunfels, Tilmann Buddensieg, Michael S. Cullen, Jörn Düwel, Helmut Engel, Ingeborg Flagge, Bruno Flierl, Max Welch Guerra, Volker Hassemer, Hans-Joachim Henzgen, Frank Hesse, Dieter Hoffmann-Axthelm, Wolfgang Kil, Daniel Libeskind, Johannes Leithäuser, Florian Mausbach, Dorothea von Moltke, Michael Mönninger, Wolfgang Schäche, Bernhard Schneider, Liselotte Schulz, Wolf Jobst Siedler, Hans Stimman, Heinrich Wefing, and Felix Zwoch.

Daniel Z. Wise, Jeremiah Riemer, Thomas R. Henschel, and Lisa Cohen read the manuscript at various stages and provided helpful suggestions for its improvement. I am especially indebted to Keith Peoples whose insights and generous criticism made this a better book. I was fortunate in having Clare Jacobson as my editor. I thank her and Kevin Lippert, publisher of Princeton Architectural Press. Above all, I am grateful for the love, encouragement, and patience of my favorite reader, my wife, Tania Taubes.

NOTES

INTRODUCTION

1 Quoted in Albert Speer, *Inside the Third Reich* (London: Sphere Books Limited, 1970), 249.

2 "Exposition Berlin: Une Capitale en Perspectives" (Paris: exhibition brochure, 19 October 1996–5 January 1997) (Bonn: Bundesministerium für Raumordnung, Bauwesen und Städtebau). All translations are my own, unless otherwise noted.

3 Hartmut Frank, "Welche Sprache sprechen Steine?" in Hartmut Frank, ed., *Faschistische Architektur: Planen und Bauen in Europa 1930 bis 1945* (Hamburg: Hans Christian Verlag, 1985), 7.

4 Hans-Michael Meyer-Sebastian, interview with author, Berlin, 18 December 1996.

5 Quoted in Timothy Garton Ash, *In Europe's Name: Germany and the Divided Continent* (London: Jonathan Cape, 1993), 23.

6 Quoted in Alan Cowell, "Kohl Casts Europe's Economic Union as War and Peace Issue," *New York Times*, 17 October 1995, A10.

7 Charles T. Goodsell, *The Social Meaning of Civic Space: Studying Political Authority through Architecture* (Lawrence, Kansas: University Press of Kansas, 1988), 8.

8 Peter Glotz, "Das Provisorium wird souverän: Der stille Aufstieg Bonns," in Uwe Schultz, ed., *Die Hauptstadt der Deutschen* (Munich: Verlag C. H. Beck, 1993), 225.

9 Quoted in Thomas Schumacher, "Giuseppe Terragni: Political and Other Allegories," in Samuel C. Kendall, ed., *The Architecture of Politics: 1910–1940* (Miami Beach, Florida: Wolfsonian Foundation, 1995), 48.

10 Goodsell, *Social Meaning of Civic Space*, 9.

11 Barbara Jakubeit, interview with author, Darmstadt, 2 November 1995.

12 Hans Klein, interview with author, Bonn, 24 October 1995.

13 Oscar Schneider, interview with author, Bonn, 24 October 1995.

14 Michael Stürmer, "Die Republik auf der Suche nach Staat und Stil," in Günter Ermisch, Hans E. Hieronymus, Werner Knopp, and Christoph Stölzl, eds., *Wanderungen durch die Kulturpolitik. Festschrift für Sieghart v. Köckritz* (Berlin: Nicolai Verlag, 1993), 17–9.

15 Mathias Schreiber, "Selbstdarstellung der Bundesrepublik Deutschland: Repräsentation des Staates in Bauten und Gedenkstätten," in Jörg-Dieter Gauger and Justin Stagl, eds., *Staatsrepräsentation* (Berlin: Dietrich Reimer Verlag, 1992), 203.

16 Peter Conradi, interview with author, Bonn, 24 October 1995.

BONN: CAPITAL OF SELF-EFFACEMENT

17 Quoted in Hermann Glaser, Lutz von Pufendorf, and Michael Schöneich, eds., *So viel Anfang war nie, Deutsche Städte 1945–1949* (Berlin: Siedler Verlag, 1989), 67.

18 Gaston Coblentz, "Letter from Bonn: Strange Capital in Europe," *New York Herald Tribune*, 19 August 1959, 14.

19 Quoted in John Dornberg, *The New Germans* (New York: Macmillan, 1975), 248.

20 Ibid.

21 Quoted in Elaine S. Hochman, *Architects of Fortune: Mies van der Rohe and the Third Reich* (New York: Weidenfeld & Nicolson, 1989), 78.

22 Mayor Rickert, quoted in Ingeborg Flagge and Wolfgang Jean Stock, eds., *Architektur und Demokratie* (Stuttgart: Hatje Verlag, 1992), 8.

23 Quoted in Claude Schnaidt, *Hannes Meyer: Buildings, Projects and Writings* (Teufen, Switzerland: Verlag Arthur Niggli, 1965), 25.

24 Quoted in Heinrich Wefing, *Parlamentsarchitektur: Zur Selbstdarstellung der Demokratie in ihren Bauwerken. Eine Untersuchung am Beispiel des Bonner Bundeshauses* (Berlin: Duncker & Humblot, 1995), 114–5.

25 Quoted in Gisbert Knopp, "Der Plenarsaal des deutschen Bundestages," in Bundesminister für Raumordnung, Bauwesen und Städtebau, ed., *Vierzig Jahre Bundeshauptstadt Bonn 1949–89* (Karlsruhe: Verlag C. F. Müller, 1989), 61.

26 Hermann Wardersleb, quoted in Wefing, *Parlamentsarchitektur*, 167.

27 Quoted in Wefing, *Parlamentsarchitektur*, 92.

28 Quoted in Wefing, *Parlamentsarchitektur*, 94.

29 Quoted in Dieter Bartetzko, "Synthesis of Fragments," in Annegret Burg and Sebastian Redecke, eds., *Chancellery and Office of the President of the Federal Republic of Germany: International Architectural Competitions for the Capital Berlin* (Berlin: Bauwelt/ Birkhäuser Verlag, 1995), 11.

30 Quoted in Dieter Bartetzko, "Seine Experimente," *Frankfurter Allgemeine Zeitung*, 4 February 1997, 37.

31 Quoted in Flagge and Stock, *Architektur und Demokratie*, 255.

32 Hans Wichmann, *Sep Ruf: Bauten und Projekte* (Stuttgart: Deutsche Verlags-Anstalt, 1986), 122.

33 Paul Betts, "The Bauhaus as Cold-War Legend: West German Modernism Revisited," *German Politics and Society* 14, no. 2 (Summer 1996): 75–91.

34 John le Carré, *A Small Town in Germany* (1968; reprint, New York: Dell, 1983), 17.

35 *Der Spiegel* (24 May 1971), quoted in Wolfgang Leuschner, *Bauten des Bundes 1965–1980* (Karlsruhe: Verlag C. F. Müller, 1980), 325.

36 I. M. Pei, interview with author, New York, 26 February 1997.

37 Quoted in Leuschner, *Bauten des Bundes*, 312.

38 Ibid., 318.

39 Günter Behnisch, interview with author, Stuttgart, 1 November 1995.

40 Ibid.

41 Peter Conradi, "Transparente Architektur =Demokratie?" *Der Architekt* 9 (September 1995): 541.

42 Quoted in Flagge and Stock, *Architektur und Demokratie*, 7.

43 Quoted in "Democracy Workshop in Glass," *Kultur-Chronik* 1 (1993): 25.

EAST BERLIN
COMMUNISM PURSUES GRANDEUR

44 Quoted in Bruno Flierl, "Bauten der 'Volksdemokratie,'" in Flagge and Stock, *Architektur und Demokratie*, 176.

45 Kurt Liebknecht, "Deutsche Architektur" *Deutsche Architektur* 1 (1952): 6.

46 Ibid.

47 "Architektonischer Aschermittwoch in Bonn," *Deutsche Architektur* 4 (1953): 207.

48 "Sixteen Principles of Urban Planning," quoted in Jörn Düwel, "Berlin: Planen im Kalten Krieg," in Marita Gleiss, ed., *Krieg-Zerstörung-Aufbau, Architekten und Stadtplanung 1940–1960* (Berlin: Henschel Verlag, 1995), 208-11.

49 *Neue Berliner Illustrierte*, 4 September 1951, quoted in Johann Friedrich Geist and Klaus Kürvers, *Das Berliner Mietshaus 1945–1989* (Munich: Prestel Verlag, 1989), 339.

50 Wolfgang Schäche, ed., *Hermann Henselmann: "Ich habe Vorschläge gemacht"* (Berlin: Ernst & Sohn, 1995), 18.

51 Quoted in Düwel, "Berlin," 230.

52 Quoted in Nicholas Bernau, "Der Ort des Souveräns," in Förderverein Berliner Stadtschloss, *Das Schloss? Eine Ausstellung über die Mitte Berlins* (Berlin: Ernst & Sohn, 1993), 75.

53 Quoted in Geist and Kürvers, *Das Berliner Mietshaus*, 322.

54 Quoted in Anders Aman, *Architecture and Ideology in Eastern Europe during the Stalin Era* (Cambridge, Massachusetts: MIT Press, 1992), 219.

55 Quoted in Josef Paul Kleihues, "From the Destruction to the Critical Reconstruction of the City: Urban Design in Berlin after 1945," in Kleihues and Christina Rathgeber, eds., *Berlin-New York: Like and Unlike* (New York: Rizzoli, 1993), 401.

56 Quoted in Anders Aman, *Architecture and Ideology*, 232-3.

57 Gerhard Kosel, *Unternehmen Wissenschaft: Die Wiederentdeckung einer Idee* (Berlin: Henschelverlag, 1989), 249-52.

58 Joachim Näther, interview with author, Berlin, 12 December 1996.

59 Ibid. Näther lives in retirement today, bitter that his life's work and experience are neglected in unified Germany. "I am unwanted," he said. "Architects are a kind of service provider. We are like tailors. A client wants a suit, you make one that fits. You don't always tell him if it looks bad. Our party leaders once had the final say; today it's the investors."

60 Gerhard Kosel, interview with author, Berlin, 20 December 1996.

61 Roland Korn, interview with author, Berlin, 17 December 1996.

62 Josef Kaiser, "Das Ministerium für Auswärtige Angelegenheiten in seinen Projektierungsstadien," *Deutsche Architektur* 11 (November 1965): 663.

63 Günter Kunert, interview with author, Berlin, 16 December 1996.

64 Kaiser, "Das Ministerium," 663.

65 Peter Schweizer, "Der Aufbau der Leipzigerstrasse in Berlin," *Deutsche Architektur* 9 (September 1969): 526.

66 Quoted in Thomas Topfstedt, *Städtebau in der DDR 1955–1971* (Leipzig: VEB E. A. Seemann Verlag, 1988), 63.

67 Heinz Graffunder, "Palast der Republik," *Architektur der DDR* (May 1976): 270.

68 Wolf Eisentraut, interview with author, Berlin, 10 December 1996. Eisentraut, now 54, is currently an architect in private practice. "It was perhaps the most exciting time of my life," he said of his work on the Palace of the Republic. On 4 October 1989, only weeks before the Berlin Wall fell, Eisentraut accepted East Germany's National Prize for Art and Literature from Prime Minister Willi Stoph for his state architectural work. Today he says, "One didn't take ideological matters very seriously. From the professional standpoint of an architect, one wanted to make a beautiful building and it was a wonderful commission. I must admit—you don't hear this much anymore about the GDR—it was a good time for me."

69 Quoted in T. H. Elkins, *Berlin: The Spatial Structure of a Divided City* (London: Methuen, 1984), 205.

MASTER PLAN FOR A GOVERNMENT DISTRICT

70 Günter Stahn, interview with author, Berlin, 4 April 1997.

71 Karen Van Langen, interview with author, New York, 16 March 1994.

72 Margaret Thatcher, *The Downing Street Years* (New York: HarperCollins, 1993), 814.

73 Quoted in Andrei S. Markovits and Simon Reich, *The German Predicament: Memory and Power in the New Europe* (Ithaca: Cornell University Press, 1997), 23.

74 Claude Vasconi, telephone interview with author, 26 May 1997.

75 Quoted in Van Langen, interview.

76 Quoted in Arbeitsgruppe Berlin-Wettbewerbe, *Hauptstadt Berlin—Parlamentsviertel im Spreebogen, Internationaler Städtebaulicher Ideenwettbewerb* (Berlin: Bauwelt/Birkhäuser Verlag, 1993), 47.

77 Transcript of Second Colloquium of the German Parliament, Berlin, 12 March 1993.

78 Ibid.

79 Axel Schultes, text of a lecture to the Schüco Forum, Berlin, 24 November 1994, 11.

80 Transcript of Second Colloquium, 9.

CHOOSING A CHANCELLERY

81 Quoted in Speer, *Inside the Third Reich*, 69.

82 Quoted in Robert R. Taylor, *The Word in Stone: The Role of Architecture in the National Socialist Ideology* (Berkeley: University of California Press, 1974), 140.

83 Hans-Achim Roll, interview with author, Bonn, 25 October 1995.

84 Quoted in "Ein undiplomatischer Diplomat," *Der Spiegel* 38 (19 September 1994): 16.

85 Klaus Harpprecht, "Der 'Teutonen-Klotz' in Washington oder: Über die Architektur der Arroganz," in Peter Neitzke, Carl Steckeweh, and Reinhart Wustlich, eds., *Centrum: Jahrbuch Architektur und Stadt* (Gütersloh: Bertelsmann Verlag, 1996), 247-9.

86 Benjamin Forgey, "German Residence Misses the Mark," *Washington Post*, 22 October 1994, C1.

87 Jörg von Uthmann, "Spiegelungen im Zierteich," *Frankfurter Allgemeine Zeitung*, 13 September 1994, 37.

88 Annegret Burg and Sebastian Redecke, eds., *Chancellery and Office of the President of the Federal Republic of Germany: International Architectural Competitions for the Capital Berlin* (Berlin: Bauwelt/Birkhäuser Verlag, 1995), 61.

89 "Wettbewerb Bundeskanzleramt," *Bauwelt* 1–2 (13 January 1995): 62.

90 Rudolf Stegers, "Drang zum Monumentalen," *Die Zeit* (30 December 1994): 14.

91 Peter Conradi, interview with author, Bonn, 24 October 1995.

92 Torsten Krüger, interview with author, Berlin, 10 October 1995.

93 Quoted in *Der Spiegel* 8 (20 February 1995): 64.

94 "Bloss nicht diese Hauptstadt! Heinrich Klotz im Gespräch mit Nikolaus Kuhnert und Angelika Schnell," *Arch+* 122 (June 1994): 25.

95 Daniel Libeskind, "Letter from Berlin," *ANY* 1, no. 6 (May/June 1994): 48.

96 Vittorio Magnago Lampugnani, "Die Provokation des Alltäglichen," *Der Spiegel* 51 (20 December 1993): 146.

97 Günter Behnisch, interview with author, Stuttgart, 1 November 1995.

98 ARD network program "Berichte aus Bonn," 24 March 1995.

99 Helmut Kohl, "Einleitende Erklärung zur Pressekonferenz von Bundeskanzler Dr. Helmut Kohl," Berlin, 28 June 1995, Presse- und Informationsamt der Bundesregierung.

100 Axel Schultes, interview with author, Berlin, 13 October 1995.

101 Axel Schultes, "Ich will einen Ort des Gleichgewichts," *Frankfurter Allgemeine Zeitung*, 29 June 1995, 29.

102 Schultes, interview.

103 Ibid.

104 Axel Schultes, interview with author, Berlin, 15 October 1996.

105 Ibid.

106 Quoted in *Die Bundesregierung zieht um* (Bonn: Presse- und Informationsamt der Bundesregierung, December 1994), 60.

107 Schultes, interview, 15 October 1996.

PRESIDENTIAL OFFICE
GLITTERING JEWEL OR DARK FORTRESS?

108 Roman Herzog, *Wahrheit und Klarheit: Reden zur deutschen Geschichte* (Hamburg: Hoffman und Campe Verlag, 1995), 23–5.

109 Andreas Gottlieb Hempel, interview with author, Berlin, 20 December 1996.

110 Helmut Kleine-Kraneburg, interview with author, Frankfurt, 31 October 1995.

111 Martin Gruber, interview with author, Frankfurt, 31 October 1995.

112 Kleine-Kraneburg, interview.

113 Walter Karschies, interview with author, Bonn, 27 October 1995.

114 Otto Meitinger, Victor Lopez Cotelo, and Helge Pitz, *Zur Fassadengestaltung des Neubaues des Bundespräsidialamtes in Berlin*, unpublished document (Berlin: Bundespräsidialamt, 23 May 1996), 2.

115 Walter Karschies, interview with author, Berlin, 18 October 1996.

116 Quoted in *Neubau des Bundespräsidialamtes* (Berlin: Presse- und Informationsamt der Bundesregierung, 1996).

NAZISM'S ARCHITECTURAL REMNANTS

117 Quoted in Taylor, *Word in Stone*, 140.

118 Dieter Hoffmann-Axthelm, "Politik, Investoren, Kultur im Streit um das Berliner

Zentrum," in Vittorio Magnago Lampugnani, ed., *Jahrbuch für Architektur, 1991* (Braunschweig: Vieweg Verlag, 1991), 37.

119 Harald Bodenschatz, Johannes Geisenhof, and Dorothea Tscheschner, *Gutachten zur bau-, stadtbau und nutzungsgeschichtlichen Bedeutung des "Hauses der Parlamentarier," (ehem. Reichsbanksgebäude bzw. ZK-Gebäude der SED), des Treuhandgebäudes ("Detlev Rohwedder Haus"), ehem. Gebäude des Reichsluftfahrtministeriums bzw. Haus der Ministerien) und des ehemaligen Staatsratsgebäudes*, unpublished manuscript (Berlin, 1993), 12.

120 Ibid., 4.

121 Quoted in Karl Hugo Pruys, *Auf dem Weg nach Berlin: Klaus Töpfer im Gespräch mit Karl Hugo Pruys* (Berlin: edition q Verlag, 1996), 22.

122 "10. Informationsblatt 'Bonn-Berlin,'" *Auswärtiges Amt, Arbeitstab Umzug Berlin*, 18 December 1992.

123 Fritjof von Nordenskjöld, interview with author, Berlin, 2 April 1997.

124 Andreas Nachama, interview with author, Berlin, 2 April 1997.

125 See John Czaplicka, "Monumental Revisions of History in Twentieth-Century Germany: An Ongoing Process," in Donald Martin Reynolds, ed., *"Remove not the Ancient Landmark": Public Monuments and Moral Values* (Amsterdam: Gordon and Breach Publishers, 1996), 141-60.

126 Hans-Michael Meyer-Sebastian, interview with author, Berlin, 18 December 1996.

127 Winfried Nerdinger, interview with author, Munich, 30 October 1995.

128 Quoted in Elaine S. Hochman, *Architects of Fortune: Mies van der Rohe and the Third Reich* (New York: Weidenfeld and Nicolson, 1989), 153.

129 Wolfgang Schäche, *Architektur und Städtebau in Berlin zwischen 1933 und 1945* (Berlin: Gebr. Mann Verlag, 1992), 160.

130 Quoted in Otto D. Tolischus, "Reichsbank Lays Base of New Home," *New York Times*, 6 May 1934, 26F.

131 William L. Shirer, *The Rise and Fall of the Third Reich* (London and Sydney: Pan Books, 1964), 1158.

132 Andreas Marx, interview with author, Berlin, 17 December 1996.

133 Shirer, *Rise and Fall*, 255.

134 Marx, interview.

135 Von Nordenskjöld, interview.

136 Barbara Jakubeit, interview with author, Berlin, 18 December 1996.

137 *Foreign Ministry Architectural Design Competition Brief* (Berlin: Federal Construction Board, 1995), 58.

138 "Hier regiert der Schlamm," *Der Spiegel* 49 (12 December 1996): 27.

139 Jakubeit, interview.

140 Thomas Müller, interview with author, Berlin, 11 October 1996.

141 Von Nordenskjöld, interview.

142 Hans Kollhoff, interview with author, Berlin, 16 October 1996.

143 Foreign Minister Klaus Kinkel, speech in Berlin, 24 August 1996.

144 Tobias Amme, interview with author, Berlin, 12 December 1996.

145 Hans-Ernst Mittig, "NS-Motive in der Gegenwartskunst: Flamme empor?" *Kritische Berichte* 2 (1989): 102.

146 Klaus Bussmann, telephone interview with author, 11 June 1997.

147 See "Neue Rechte am Bau?" *Der Spiegel* 45 (6 November 1995): 244–55.

148 Kollhoff, interview.

149 Quoted in Taylor, *Word in Stone*, 197.

150 Ibid., 196

151 Ibid., 197.

152 Ibid., 196.

153 Günter Grass, *Ein weites Feld* (Göttingen: Steidl Verlag, 1995), 66.

154 Werner Durth, *Deutsche Architekten: Biographische Verflechtungen 1900–1970* (Braunschweig: Friedrich Vieweg und Sohn Verlagsgesellschaft, 1986), 138.

155 Wolfgang Keilholz, interview with author, Berlin, 13 December 1996.

156 Helge Pitz, interview with author, Berlin, 27 March 1997.

157 Wolfgang Keilholz, interview with author, Berlin, 27 March 1997.

158 Christine Hoh-Slodczyk, interview with author, Berlin, 27 March 1997.

159 Keilholz, interview, 13 December 1996.

160 Ibid. In this context, it is interesting to note that the United States Consulate in West Berlin has long occupied another Nazi-era military complex designed by Sagebiel, the former Luftwaffe Command Headquarters for eastern Germany.

161 Quoted in Karl Hugo Pruys, *Auf dem Weg*, 98.

COMMUNIST RELICS

162 Manfred Sack, "Introduction," in Gerhard G. Feldmeyer, *The New German Architecture* (New York: Rizzoli, 1993), 18–9.

163 Philip Johnson, "Berlin's Last Chance—Schinkel, Messel, Mies van der Rohe—Now What," 13 June 1993, text of speech provided by architect's office.

164 Klaus Hartung, "Der Hauptstadt Plan: Operation am offenen Herzen," *Die Zeit*, 6 December 1996, 7.

165 Quoted in Harald Bodenschatz, ed., *Eine Zukunft für das Ehemalige Staatsrats-gebäude!* (Berlin: Architektenkammer Berlin and the Deutscher Werkbund Berlin, January 1995), 1.

166 Harald Bodenschatz, telephone interview with author, 17 March 1997.

167 Bodenschatz, Geisenhof, and Tscheschner, *Gutachten zur bau-*, 10.

168 Quoted in "Erster Spatenstich für den Neubau des Kanzleramtes in Berlin," *Frankfurter Allgemeine Zeitung*, 5 February 1997, 1.

169 *BZ*, 4 May 1995, quoted in Harald Bodenschatz, *"Der Rote Kasten": zu Bedeutung, Wirkung und Zukunft von Schinkels Bauakademie* (Berlin: Transit Buchverlag, 1996), 18.

170 Annette Ahme, interview with author, Berlin, 31 March 1997.

171 Quoted in Marc Fisher, *After the Wall: Germany, the Germans and the Burdens of History* (New York: Simon & Schuster, 1995), 73.

172 Arbeitsgruppe Berlin-Wettbewerbe, *Hauptstadt Berlin—Stadtmitte Spreeinsel: Internationaler Städtebaulicher Ideenwettbewerb 1994* (Berlin: Bauwelt/Birkhäuser Verlag, 1994), 146–7.

173 Jakubeit, interview.

174 Ibid.

175 Dieter Hoffmann-Axthelm, "City and

State in Midtown Berlin," (English text) in Arbeitsgruppe Berlin-Wettbewerbe, *Hauptstadt Berlin*, 15.

176 Brian Ladd, *The Ghosts of Berlin: Confronting German History in the Urban Landscape* (Chicago: University of Chicago Press, 1997), 47-70.

177 Program notes for "Rock für den Frieden," January 1984.

178 Joachim Fest, "Plädoyer für den Wiederaufbau des Stadtschlosses," in Michael Mönninger, ed., *Das Neue Berlin: Baugeschichte und Stadtplanung der deutschen Hauptstadt* (Frankfurt: Insel Verlag, 1991), 118.

179 President Roman Herzog, speech in Magdeburg, 31 May 1995, quoted in *Bulletin* 47 (Bonn: Presse- und Informationsamt der Bundesregierung, 8 June 1995): 419.

NORMAN FOSTER'S REICHSTAG ILLUMINATING SHADOWS OF THE PAST

180 Günter Behnisch, testimony in transcript of Reichstag Colloquium, Berlin, 15 February 1992, 45.

181 Oscar Schneider, "Denkmal der Demokratie," *Frankfurter Allgemeine Zeitung*, 18 April 1994, 33.

182 Quoted in Michael S. Cullen, *Der Reichstag: Die Geschichte eines Monumentes* (Stuttgart: Parkland Verlag, 1990), 32.

183 Tilmann Buddensieg, *Berliner Labyrinth* (Berlin: Verlag Klaus Wagenbach, 1993), 77-80.

184 Cullen, *Der Reichstag*, 314-7.

185 Peter Conradi, Bundestag debate, 25 February 1994, reprinted in *Deutscher Bundestag: Verhüllter Reichstag—Projekt für Berlin* (Bonn: Deutscher Bundestag Referat Öffentlichkeitsarbeit, 1995), 18276.

186 Michael Mönninger, quoted in *Bauwelt* 14/15 (9 April 1993): 771.

187 Dietmar Kansy, interview with author, Bonn, 24 October 1995.

188 Sir Norman Foster and Partners, *Reichstag Berlin* (exhibition catalog) (Berlin: Aedes Gallery, August 1994), 8.

189 Ibid., 12.

190 Oscar Schneider, interview with author, Bonn, 24 October 1995.

191 Sir Norman Foster, statement at Second Competition Stage of Reichstag Competition, June 1993.

192 "Zurück in die Zukunft," *Bauwelt* 27 (15 July 1994): 1523.

193 Quoted in "Hier regiert der Schlamm," *Der Spiegel* 49 (12 December 1996): 33.

194 George A. Dudley, *A Workshop for Peace: Designing the United Nations Headquarters* (Cambridge, Massachusetts: Architectural History Foundation/ MIT Press, 1994), 223.

195 William C. Allen, *The Dome of the United States Capitol: An Architectural History* (Washington, D.C.: U.S. Government Printing Office, 1992), 5.

196 Foster, *Reichstag Berlin*, 30.

197 Mark Braun, Sir Norman Foster and Partners Reichstag project director, interview with author, Berlin, 12 December 1996.

198 Ibid.

199 Quoted in Karl Schlögl, "Die Kuppel des Reichstags," in *Mythos Berlin: zur Wahrnehmungsgeschichte einer industrielle Metropole*, exhibition catalog (Berlin: Ästhetik und Kommunikation, 1987), 98.

200 "Durch den Regen," *Der Spiegel* 12 (20 March 1995): 21.

201 Adolf Hitler, *Mein Kampf*, trans. Ralph Manheim (1943; reprint, Boston: Houghton Mifflin, 1971), 265–6.

202 Michael S. Cullen, "Man stelle sich vor: Der deutsche Parlamentarier im Paletot des Kaisers!" *Frankfurter Allgemeine Zeitung*, 4 December 1996, 41.

203 Quoted in Deyan Sudjic, *Norman Foster, Richard Rogers, James Stirling: New Directions in British Architecture* (London: Thames and Hudson, 1986), 54.

I. M. PEI AND A PRUSSIAN INHERITANCE

204 William L. Shirer, *End of a Berlin Diary* (New York: Alfred A. Knopf, 1947), 142.

205 Quoted in Regina Müller, *Das Berliner Zeughaus: Die Baugeschichte* (Berlin: Brandenburgisches Verlagshaus, 1994), 249.

206 Translation from Robert R. Taylor, *Hohenzollern Berlin: Construction and Reconstruction* (Port Credit, Ontario: P. D. Meany Publishers, 1985), 44.

207 Quoted in Müller, *Das Berliner Zeughaus*, 227.

208 Quoted in Harold James, *A German Identity: 1770–1990* (New York: Routledge, 1989), 204.

209 Christoph Stölzl, interview with author, Berlin, 20 October 1995.

210 Ibid. The exhibition has been questioned by critics who argue that it overlooks what they see as Germany's unique, fatally flawed, historical trajectory outside liberalizing trends elsewhere on the continent. See Peter Reichel, *Politik mit der Erinnerung: Gedächtnisorte im Streit um die Nationalsozialistische Vergangenheit* (Munich: Carl Hanser Verlag, 1995), 253–7.

211 I. M. Pei, interview with author, New York, 26 February 1997.

212 Quoted in Heinrich Wefing, "Pei bleibt Pei: Sein Erweiterungsbau zum Deutschen Historischen Museum Berlin," *Frankfurter Allgemeine Zeitung*, 20 January 1997, 27.

213 Quoted in Ian Buruma, *The Wages of Guilt: Memories of War in Germany and Japan* (New York: Farrar Straus & Giroux, 1994), 236.

214 Pei, interview.

215 Ibid.

216 Christoph Stölzl, interview with author, Berlin, 3 April 1997.

217 Pei, interview.

218 Gottfried Knapp, "Aus der Mantel der Geschichte: Wie sich Pei das 'Schauhaus' des Deutschen Historischen Museums in Berlin vorstellt," *Süddeutsche Zeitung*, 21 January 1997.

MONUMENTS TO VICTIMS, NOT HEROES

219 Helmut Kohl, remarks in Bundestag debate on 14 May 1993, quoted in Christoph Stölzl, ed., *Die Neue Wache Unter den Linden: ein deutsches Denkmal im Wandel der Geschichte* (Berlin: Koehler & Amelang, 1993), 214.

220 Quoted in Reichel, *Politik mit der Erinnerung*, 242.

221 "Das Gedenken nicht zentralisieren," *Frankfurter Allgemeine Zeitung*, 11 April 1997, 5.

222 Quoted in *Denkmal für die ermordeten Juden Europas, Künstlerischer Wettbewerb,*

Kurzdokumentation (Berlin: Senats-verwaltung für Bau und Wohnungs-wesen, 1995), entry 1456.

223 Henryk M. Broder, "Deutschmeister des Trauens," *Der Spiegel* 16 (17 April 1995): 222.

224 "Gespräch mit Ignatz Bubis: Millionen Namen sind nicht Genug," *Frankfurter Allgemeine Zeitung*, 29 July 1995, 29.

225 James E. Young, telephone interview with author, 7 December 1997.

226 Press Release, "Berlin Senatsverwaltung für Wissenschaft, Forschung und Kultur, Recommendation by the Findungs-kommission for Berlin's Memorial to Europe's Murdered Jews, 16 November 1997," English-language text.

227 James E. Young, "Germany's Memorial Question: Memory, Counter-memory and the End of the Monument," paper prepared for the Third Colloquium on the Memorial to the Murdered Jews of Europe, Berlin, 11 April 1997.

HESITATION BY DESIGN

228 Hans Klein, interview with author, Bonn, 24 October 1995.

229 Quoted in Rainer Stache, "Vernich-tendes Architekten-Urteil über neues Berlin: Die Seele fehlt," *Berliner Morgenpost*, 17 January 1996.

230 Quoted in Hans Stimman, ed., *Babylon, Berlin etc.: Das Vokabular der europäischen Stadt* (Basel: Birkhäuser Verlag, 1995), 35.

231 Ibid., 83.

232 Quoted in Knopp, "Der Plenarsaal," 61.

LIST OF SOURCES

Allen, William C. *The Dome of the United States Capitol: An Architectural History.* Washington, D.C.: U.S. Government Printing Office, 1992.

Aman, Anders. *Architecture and Ideology in Eastern Europe during the Stalin Era.* Cambridge, Massachusetts: MIT Press, 1992.

Arbeitsgruppe Berlin-Wettbewerbe. Hauptstadt Berlin—Parlamentsviertel im Spreebogen, Internationaler Städtebaulicher Ideenwettbewerb 1993. Berlin: Bauwelt/Birkhäuser Verlag, 1993.

Arbeitsgruppe Berlin-Wettbewerbe. *Hauptstadt Berlin—Stadtmitte Spreeinsel, Internationaler Städtebaulicher Ideenwettbewerb 1994.* Berlin: Bauwelt/Birkhäuser Verlag, 1994.

"Architektonischer Aschermittwoch in Bonn" *Deutsche Architektur* 4 (1953).

Balfour, Allan. *Berlin: The Politics of Order, 1737–1989.* New York: Rizzoli, 1990.

Betts, Paul. "The Bauhaus as Cold-War Legend: West German Modernism Revisited." *German Politics and Society* 14, no. 2 (Summer 1996): 75–91.

"Bloss nicht diese Hauptstadt! Heinrich Klotz im Gespräch mit Nikolaus Kuhnert und Angelika Schnell." *Arch+* 122 (June 1994): 23–7.

Bodenschatz, Harald. *"Der Rote Kasten": zu Bedeutung, Wirkung und Zukunft von Schinkels Bauakademie.* Berlin: Transit Buchverlag, 1996.

Bodenschatz, Harald, ed. *Eine Zukunft für das Ehemalige Staatsratsgebäude!* Berlin: Architektenkammer Berlin and the Deutscher Werkbund Berlin (January 1995).

Bodenschatz, Harald, Johannes Geisenhof, and Dorothea Tscheschner. *Gutachten zur bau-, stadtbau und nutzungsgeschichtlichen Bedeutung des "Hauses der Parlamentarier," (ehem. Reichsbanksgebäude bzw. ZK-Gebäude der SED), des Treuhandgebäudes ("Detlev Rohwedder Haus"), ehem. Gebäude des Reichsluftfahrtministeriums bzw. Haus der Ministerien) und des ehemaligen Staatsratsgebäudes.* Unpublished manuscript. Berlin, 1993.

Broder, Henryk M. "Deutschmeister des Trauens." *Der Spiegel* 16 (17 April 1995): 222–4.

Buddensieg, Tilmann. *Berliner Labyrinth.* Berlin: Verlag Klaus Wagenbach, 1993.

Bundesminister für Raumordnung, Bauwesen und Städtebau, ed. *Vierzig Jahre Bundeshauptstadt Bonn 1949–89.* Karlsruhe: Verlag C. F. Müller, 1989.

Burg, Annegret and Sebastian Redecke, eds. *Chancellery and Office of the President of the Federal Republic of Germany: International Architectural Competitions for the Capital Berlin.* Berlin: Bauwelt/Birkhäuser Verlag, 1995.

Buruma, Ian. *The Wages of Guilt: Memories of War in Germany and Japan.* New York: Farrar Straus & Giroux, 1994.

Conradi, Peter. "Bewirkt Transparente Architektur=Demokratie?" *Der Architekt* 9 (September 1995): 539-42.

Cotelo, Victor Lopez, Otto Meitinger, and Helge Pitz. *Zur Fassadengestaltung des Neubaues des Bundespräsidialamtes in Berlin.* Unpublished document. Berlin: 23 May 1996.

Cullen, Michael S. *Der Reichstag: Die Geschichte eines Monumentes.* Stuttgart: Parkland Verlag, 1990.

"Democracy Workshop in Glass." *Kultur-Chronik* 1 (1993): 25-8.

Denkmal für die ermordeten Juden Europas, Künstlerischer Wettbewerb, Kurzdokumentation. Berlin: Berlin Senate Building and Housing and Authority, 1995.

Die Bundesregierung zieht um. Bonn: Presse- und Informationsamt der Bundesregierung, December 1994.

Dornberg, John. *The New Germans.* New York: Macmillan, 1975.

Dudley, George A. *A Workshop for Peace: Designing the United Nations Headquarters.* Cambridge, Massachusetts: Architectural History Foundation/MIT Press, 1994.

"Durch den Regen." *Der Spiegel* 12 (20 March 1995): 20-1.

Durth, Werner. *Deutsche Architekten: Biographische Verflechtungen 1900–1970.* Braunschweig: Friedrich Vieweg und Sohn Verlagsgesellschaft, 1986.

"Ein undiplomatischer Diplomat." *Der Spiegel* 38 (19 September 1994): 16.

Elkins, T. H. *Berlin: The Spatial Structure of a Divided City.* London: Methuen, 1984.

Ermisch, Günter, Hans E. Hieronymus, Werner Knopp, Christoph Stölzl, eds. *Wanderungen durch die Kulturpolitik.*

Festschrift für Sieghart v. Köckritz. Berlin: Nicolai Verlag, 1993.

Feldmeyer, Gerhard G. *The New German Architecture.* New York: Rizzoli, 1993.

Fisher, Marc. *After the Wall: Germany, the Germans and the Burdens of History.* New York: Simon & Schuster, 1995.

Flagge, Ingeborg and Wolfgang Jean Stock, eds. *Architektur und Demokratie.* Stuttgart: Hatje Verlag, 1992.

Förderverein Berliner Stadtschloss. *Das Schloss? Eine Ausstellung über die Mitte Berlins.* Berlin: Ernst & Sohn, 1993.

Foreign Ministry Architectural Design Competition Brief. Berlin: Federal Construction Board, 1995.

Foster, Sir Norman and Partners. *Reichstag Berlin* (exhibition catalog). Berlin: Aedes Gallery, August 1994.

Frank, Hartmut, ed. *Faschistische Architektur: Planen und Bauen in Europa 1930 bis 1945.* Hamburg: Hans Christian Verlag, 1985.

Garton Ash, Timothy. *In Europe's Name: Germany and the Divided Continent.* London: Jonathan Cape, 1993.

Gauger, Jörg-Dieter and Justin Stagl, eds. *Staatsrepräsentation.* Berlin: Dietrich Reimer Verlag, 1992.

Geist, Johann Friedrich and Klaus Kürvers, eds. *Das Berliner Mietshaus 1945–1989.* Munich: Prestel Verlag, 1989.

Glaser, Hermann, Lutz von Pufendorf, and Michael Schöneich, eds. *So viel Anfang war nie, Deutsche Städte 1945–1949.* Berlin: Siedler Verlag, 1989.

Gleiss, Marita, ed. *Krieg-Zerstörung-Aufbau, Architekten und Stadtplanung 1940–1960.* Berlin: Henschel Verlag, 1995.

Goodsell, Charles T. *The Social Meaning of Civic Space: Studying Political Authority through Architecture.* Lawrence, Kansas: University Press of Kansas, 1988.

Graffunder, Heinz. "Palast der Republik." *Architektur der DDR* (May 1976): 265-71.

Grass, Günter. *Ein weites Feld.* Göttingen: Steidl Verlag, 1995.

Herzog, Roman. *Wahrheit und Klarheit; Reden zur deutschen Geschichte.* Hamburg: Hoffman und Campe Verlag, 1995.

"Hier regiert der Schlamm." *Der Spiegel* 49 (12 December 1996): 22-34.

Hitler, Adolf. *Mein Kampf.* Trans. Ralph Manheim. 1943. Reprint. Boston: Houghton Mifflin, 1971.

Hochman, Elaine S. *Architects of Fortune: Mies van der Rohe and the Third Reich.* New York: Weidenfeld & Nicolson, 1989.

James, Harold. *A German Identity: 1770–1990.* New York: Routledge, 1989.

Johnson, Philip. "Berlin's Last Chance—Schinkel, Messel, Mies van der Rohe—Now What." Berlin speech, 13 June 1993. Provided by architect's office.

Jones, Peter Blundell. "Der Bundestag." *Architectural Review* 93, no. 1153 (March 1993): 20-33.

Kaiser, Josef. "Das Ministerium für Auswärtige Angelegenheiten in seinen Projektierungsstadien." *Deutsche Architektur* 11 (November 1965): 655-65.

Kendall, Samuel C., ed. *The Architecture of Politics: 1910–1940.* Miami Beach, Florida: Wolfsonian Foundation, 1995.

Kleihues, Josef Paul and Christina Rathgeber, eds. *Berlin-New York: Like and Unlike.* New York: Rizzoli, 1993.

Kohl, Helmut. "Einleitende Erklärung zur Pressekonferenz von Bundeskanzler Dr. Helmut Kohl," Berlin, 28 June 1995, Presse- und Informationsamt der Bundesregierung.

Kosel, Gerhard. *Unternehmen Wissenschaft: Die Wiederentdeckung einer Idee.* Berlin: Henschelverlag, 1989.

Kramer, Jane. *The Politics of Memory: Looking for Germany in the New Germany.* New York: Random House, 1996.

Ladd, Brian. *The Ghosts of Berlin: Confronting German History in the Urban Landscape.* Chicago: University of Chicago Press, 1997.

Lampugnani, Vittorio Magnago. "Die Provokation des Alltäglichen." *Der Spiegel* 51 (20 December 1993): 142-7.

———. *Jahrbuch für Architektur, 1991.* Braunschweig: Vieweg Verlag, 1991.

Lane, Barbara Miller. *Architecture and Politics in Germany 1918–1945.* Cambridge, Massachusetts: Harvard University Press, 1985.

le Carré, John. *A Small Town in Germany.* 1968; reprint, New York: Dell, 1983.

Leuschner, Wolfgang. *Bauten des Bundes 1965–1980.* Karlsruhe: Verlag C.F. Müller, 1980.

Libeskind, Daniel. "Letter from Berlin." *ANY* 1, no. 6 (May/June 1994): 48-9.

Liebknecht, Kurt. "Deutsche Architektur." *Deutsche Architektur* 1 (1952): 6-12.

Markovits, Andrei S. and Simon Reich. *The German Predicament: Memory and Power in the New Europe.* Ithaca: Cornell University Press, 1997.

Mittig, Hans-Ernst. "NS-Motive in der Gegenwartskunst: Flamme empor?" *Kritische Berichte* 2 (1989): 91-109.

Mönninger, Michael, ed., *Das Neue Berlin: Baugeschichte und Stadtplanung der deutschen Hauptstadt*. Frankfurt: Insel Verlag, 1991.

Müller, Regina. *Das Berliner Zeughaus: Die Baugeschichte*. Berlin: Brandenburgisches Verlagshaus, 1994.

Mythos Berlin: zur Wahrnehmungsgeschichte einer industrielle Metropole (exhibition catalog). Berlin: Ästhetik und Kommunikation, 1987.

Neitzke, Peter, Carl Steckeweh, and Reinhart Wustlich, eds. *Centrum: Jahrbuch Architektur und Stadt*. Gütersloh: Bertelsmann Verlag, 1996.

Neubau des Bundespräsidialamtes (brochure). Bonn: Presse- und Informationsamt der Bundesregierung, 1996.

"Neue Rechte am Bau?" *Der Spiegel* 45 (6 November 1995): 244-55.

Pruys, Karl Hugo. *Auf dem Weg nach Berlin: Klaus Töpfer im Gespräch mit Karl Hugo Pruys*. Berlin: edition q Verlag, 1996.

Reichel, Peter. *Politik mit der Erinnerung: Gedächtnisorte im Streit um die Nationalsozialistische Vergangenheit*. Munich: Carl Hanser Verlag, 1995.

Reynolds, Donald Martin, ed. *"Remove not the Ancient Landmark": Public Monuments and Moral Values*. Amsterdam: Gordon and Breach Publishers, 1996.

Rogier, Francesa. "Growing Pains: From the Opening of the Wall to the Wrapping of the Reichstag." *Assemblage* 29 (1996): 44-71.

Schäche, Wolfgang. *Architektur und Städtebau in Berlin zwischen 1933 und 1945*. Berlin: Gebr. Mann Verlag, 1992.

————, ed. *Hermann Henselmann: "Ich habe Vorschläge gemacht."* Berlin: Ernst & Sohn, 1995.

Schnaidt, Claude. *Hannes Meyer: Buildings, Projects and Writings*. Teufen, Switzerland: Verlag Arthur Niggli, 1965.

Schultes, Axel. Lecture to Schüco Forum. Berlin: 24 November 1994.

Schultz, Uwe, ed. *Die Hauptstadt der Deutschen*. Munich: Verlag C. H. Beck, 1993.

Schweizer, Peter. "Der Aufbau der Leipzigerstrasse in Berlin." *Deutsche Architektur* 9 (September 1969): 526-9.

Senatsverwaltung für Stadtentwicklung und Umweltschutz. *Hauptstadtplanung und Denkmalpflege: Die Standorte für Parlament und Regierung in Berlin*. Berlin: Verlag Schelzky & Jeep, 1995.

Shirer, William L. *End of a Berlin Diary*. New York: Alfred A. Knopf, 1947.

————. *The Rise and Fall of the Third Reich*. London: Pan Books, 1964.

Speer, Albert. *Inside the Third Reich*. London: Sphere Books Limited, 1970.

Stimman, Hans, ed. *Babylon, Berlin etc.: Das Vokabular der europäischen Stadt*. Basel: Birkhäuser Verlag, 1995.

Stölzl, Christoph, ed. *Die Neue Wache Unter den Linden: ein deutsches Denkmal im Wandel der Geschichte*. Berlin: Koehler & Amelang, 1993.

Sudjic, Deyan. *Norman Foster, Richard Rogers, James Stirling: New Directions in British Architecture*. London: Thames and Hudson, 1986.

Taylor, Robert R. *Hohenzollern Berlin: Construction and Reconstruction*. Port Credit, Ontario: P. D. Meany Publishers, 1985.

————. *The Word in Stone: The Role of Architecture in the National Socialist Ideology*. Berkeley: University of California Press, 1974.

Thatcher, Margaret. *The Downing Street Years*. New York: HarperCollins, 1993.

Topfstedt, Thomas. *Städtebau in der DDR 1955–1971*. Leipzig: VEB E. A. Seemann Verlag, 1988.

Transcript of Bundestag debate, 25 February 1994. Reprinted in *Deutscher Bundestag: Verhüllter Reichstag—Projekt für Berlin*. Bonn: Deutscher Bundestag Referat Öffentlichkeitsarbeit, 1995.

Transcript of Reichstag Colloquium, Berlin. Bonn: Deutscher Bundestag, Stenographischer Dienst, 14–15 February 1992.

Transcript of Second Colloquium of the German Parliament, Berlin. Bonn: Deutscher Bundestag, Stenographischer Dienst, 12–13 March 1993.

Vale, Lawrence J. *Architecture, Power and National Identity*. New Haven: Yale University Press, 1992.

Wefing, Heinrich. *Parlamentsarchitektur: Zur Selbstdarstellung der Demokratie in ihren Bauwerken. Eine Untersuchung am Beispiel des Bonner Bundeshauses*. Berlin: Duncker & Humblot, 1995.

Welch Guerra, Max. "Von Bonn nach Berlin: Die Hauptstadtplanung der Berliner Republik." *RaumPlanung* 73 (June 1996): 83–91.

Wenk, Silke. *Ein "Altar des Vaterlandes" für die neue Hauptstadt? Zur Kontroverse um das "Denkmal für die ermordeten Juden Europas."* Frankfurt: Fritz Bauer Institut, 1996.

"Wettbewerb Bundeskanzleramt." *Bauwelt* 1–2 (13 January 1995): 62–5.

Wichmann, Hans. *Sep Ruf: Bauten und Projekte*. Stuttgart: Deutsche Verlags-Anstalt, 1986.

Wistrich, Robert S. *Weekend in Munich: Art, Propaganda and Terror in the Third Reich*. London: Pavilion Books, 1996.

Young, James E. "Germany's Memorial Question: Memory, Counter-memory and the End of the Monument." Paper prepared for the Third Colloquium on the Memorial to the Murdered Jews of Europe, Berlin, 11 April 1997.

"Zurück in die Zukunft." *Bauwelt* 27 (15 July 1994): 1523.

INDEX

B

World War II, 23
    Allied bombing during, 41, 84

Y

Young, James E.:
    and Holocaust memorial, 152–3, 154

Z

Zeughaus (Royal Arsenal), 135–51
    under East Germany, 135–6
    as German Historical Museum, 137–41